neighborly

THE PRACTICE *of* BIBLICAL LOVE

Kindra Gunn

FREILING PUBLISHING

Published by Freiling Publishing,
a division of Freiling Agency, LLC.

P.O. Box 1264, Warrenton, VA 20188

www.FreilingPublishing.com

ISBN: 978-1-950948-69-7

Printed in the United States of America

To Mom and Cathina
Without whom this book wouldn't have been possible.
Thank you for your strength and encouragement.

CONTENTS

1

LOVING OUR NEIGHBOR

Time crawled by silently as the cool glass of the window warmed under the skin of my forehead while I leaned against the window. Cars outside zoomed by us or kept pace with us while I carefully avoided everyone else in the car with me. The only noise was the constant humming that accompanies any vehicle driving down an interstate. The two Nintendo handheld Game Boy consoles were being used by my brother and sister while the baby slept in the car seat, and I was sitting, all by myself, in the front seat next to Mom, who was driving. Again, we were going to a place we had never seen before to be surrounded by people we didn't know as we tried to start over one more time. So, I did the only thing I could think of: I watched the people in the other cars and wondered about their lives.

I wondered if the lady next to us had children, if she was going to the grocery store or home from work or something else entirely. Maybe she was driving across the country like us or maybe she had that perfect life we saw on television. Or she could be doing something else entirely. Maybe she was loved; maybe she was lonely. Perhaps her life was wrought with adventure, or perhaps it was engulfed by trauma the likes of which a child could never understand. I wondered how many people were in her life who might love her, and then I remembered that I was supposed to love her as well. But how could I love her? I hadn't said a word to her or she to me. Chances are that we would never speak. We were somewhere on this road in Wyoming, and we weren't likely to stop anywhere here. How could I love her? I watched as she exited the freeway and we continued on our way, but the questions continued running around my mind even to the point of my maturing into adulthood.

Love is perhaps one of the most confusing and difficult concepts we struggle to understand. It's even harder to understand it as the Lord would have us understand it. As a word, the connotations are always positive, but the sometimes-apparent end result isn't always great. Defining love is an almost impossible task as so many people connect it to direct experiences from their life rather than the objective definition of love. Also, our understanding of love is often colored by the shortcomings, the traumas, the burdens, and the spiritual darkness of this world. Truly grasping the depth and beauty of love, whether it's the amazing love of God for us or the love we are supposed to have for our fellow man, can be a daunting task. Perhaps the best place to start is to form a definition or understanding of the basics of love.

What is Love?

As an English teacher, I have found that, at best, definitions for love are vague, and more commonly, tend to be circular. Rather than defining love, we describe the results of love in the same way that many of my students define a comma or as scientists define gravity. Most students come into the classroom with the thought that *commas are used to show a pause in a sentence* when the truth is much different just as most of us as humans come to others with one of two definitions for love: the first that *love is a feeling* and the other that *love is an action*. Both definitions while not wholly incorrect still only focus on the results of love rather than the foundation of it. Such definitions lead people to always feel like they are guessing. In the case of a comma, they're left making "educated guesses" about where a comma might actually belong in any given sentence based on where they think a pause should be, but in reality, that definition is unreliable and generally useless because it defines the topic (comma) with the symptom (a pause) instead of the cause. Commas have very specific purposes—too many to list here. The pause is a symptom of the comma, not its definition.

In the case of love, it leaves us without a direction to follow. We have been taught that *love is the good feeling we have towards people or things* or that *love is made up of actions of good will towards others* or even more often that *when a person hurts us, that's a sign that they must not love us*. Much like a comma's definition, it's not inaccurate, but it's a circular definition since it is defined by the visible symptoms of love instead of the cause.

Prior to my people-watching in the car that day driving across the Midwest, I had a fight with my sister over whose turn it was to play on the Game Boy, and my mother had reminded me that *we are to love our neighbor as ourselves* (Lv. 19:18, 34; Pr. 10:12, Mt. 19:19; 22:39; Mk 12:31; Lk 10:27; Jn 13:34; Ro. 12:10; 13:8-10; Gal 5:14; I Th 4:9-10; Jas 2:8; I Pet 4:8; I Jn 3:11, 14, 23; 4:7, 11, 21; 2 Jn 1:5). That set me on the journey down the path to working out a clear definition of what it means to be loving towards everyone and how we could love someone we didn't know, or even more challenging, how we could love our enemies. At the age of ten, I had defined love as a simple feeling, and the result was that I had no idea how to force myself to feel that towards people I didn't know or, even more so, towards people I didn't like. So, I was left asking myself whether it was possible, and more importantly, how could I do that. Sadly, it was many years before I found my answer.

This command deeply impacted me and often required that I evaluate it to determine what I was actually being told to do because, as a child, my life was less than ideal. At different points in time, I have been the victim of various types of tragedy; some the result of living in a fallen world such as when my father passed, and some the direct result of others' hate or malice. How could I make myself feel love towards those people who had deliberately, and with forethought, caused me and the people closest to me to feel such overwhelming and all-encompassing pain?

Obviously, advice came in various forms and from a wide-range of places that told me to "forgive for your own sake" or to "keep forgiving them every time it comes to your mind" or to "let it go" or to "change your focus" (which seemed a frivolous way of calling a person selfish or prideful because they struggle with something).

Everyone's advice was to "forgive" the person, but they never took the time to explain how. For a ten-year-old sitting in the hot car after fighting with her sister, or for the adult who struggled with abuse and loss in her past, none of that worked. And the even bigger idea that we're supposed to love these people seemed even more impossible. For the one who was hurting deep inside the soul, there seemed to be no way to reach the pain, much less to heal it. Instead, it seemed an unreachable goal. As I will talk about more in the chapter on forgiveness, I found the only way to forgive these people who had hurt me and those I love was to learn to love them, but first, I had to have a clear definition of love.

However, love was a concept that had no concrete definition, no concrete method, and no concrete meaning that anyone was able to share with me. I have always lived in the concrete world. God was concrete, I could see Him in the world, but love was a vaporous feeling that was uncontrollable and unpredictable, and I found myself completely incapable of *loving* these people as I had been commanded to. I tried various things in my life from crying alone and hiding from the pain to countless hours of begging to just forget to therapy—both Christian and secular—and yet, nothing appeared to work. I couldn't make myself forgive or love these people.

As God has brought me closer to Him and time separated me from my traumas, I found myself wanting to seek Him more earnestly. I still carried the burden of the past, but I was used to the weight and able to at least attempt walking forward. My sister, Cathina, and I teamed up to start reading and/or listening to various books that would position God as the main focus for our lives. We would meet up and talk about some of the things we had read and what we thought about them. These discussions ranged in topic from eschatology to Jewish culture to the beatitudes to the times of Christ and so much more. But the most memorable of these conversations focused on one of the shortest books we've read to date: C. S. Lewis's *The Great Divorce* (*if* you haven't read it, I highly recommend it).

The story follows a spirit, voiced in the first person as C.S. Lewis himself, who tags along from what is, in essence, hell, as a group of spirits have the opportunity to leave there and visit heaven on a special day. Lewis is emotionally detached and more interested in observing the spirits around him than he is in actively taking part—at least until the end. One of the spirits he observes is a woman from hell who is approached by the spirit of her brother from heaven. Her brother is trying to convince her to let go of her love for her son, Michael, who died very young, and to love God. The promise is that if she can let go of her love for her son, she will get to see him, but if her goal is only to see her son, she will be unable to go to where her son is—presumably with Christ. She, on the other hand, would prefer to drag her son to hell with her rather than to let go of her love for him.

One of the unspoken points of this passage seems to be that we can, in fact, love something or someone too much. Our conversation focused mostly on that concept, and the conclusion we came to was that everyone has a throne in their heart, and we all put something in that throne. Whatever it is we place on the throne of our hearts is what we love—whether it be ourselves, our possessions, a particular person, an idol, or something else entirely. When we put something there besides God, our love for it becomes obsessive and dangerous, and we begin to view everything around us through the lens of what is on that throne including the people in our lives. However, if we put God on that throne, then everything else falls into place. We look at the "things" that we possess through the lens of eternity—they're nice now, but I don't need them. We look at people as souls that need to be rescued and helped. We look to God as our guiding light. It was this conversation that set me down the right path that led to my answer.

Consider the child of a narcissist. Often, those children, if they work through all of their baggage, learn to understand that their mother or father loved them, but that love was broken by the parent's own brokenness. Narcissists are incapable of loving their children except through the lens of loving themselves first. Children of narcissists often have to learn how to love from scratch because they never experienced what real love was.

I mentally "chewed" on this book, especially this particular episode, for a long time as I continued working through my own issues. And as I considered it and all of its implications, I considered my own heart and what was sitting there. With some self-reflection, I realized that I had, in a sense, treasured my trauma as the defining characteristic of who I was. I had to change that. And with some prayer and a clear goal. I was able to. I wanted to place God in the center of my heart. With this desire to change, slowly, I found myself changing.

It wasn't too long later that on a bright Sunday morning, as I was sitting in church near the end of communion, I found myself watching the elders walk back to the front of the building carrying the trays with the leftover wine and grape juice. The sun light bounced from the windows off the liquid and the light danced across the ceiling, and slightly entranced by the dance, I thought about the sermon that day and my own life. Our pastor had spent the time talking about the "everyday" Christian, but in a sense completely different than I had heard it before; he spoke about it in a much more concrete sense. He talked about how everything from laundry to our commute to work is a good work that should be done to and for Christ. While I had heard this idea many times in my life, something about it seemed to mix with the conversation my sister and I had some time before. The idea of the throne in our hearts as well as my own realization about my own heart flowed through my mind like an ever-flowing stream of thought. As the lights settled back to stillness, I was hit by what seemed to be a simple, but life-changing, epiphany; I realized that the burden was gone—not because I somehow miraculously forgave people who had hurt me, but because I began looking at my offenders through the lens of God. Suddenly, it made sense. Later, I will talk more about this moment and what led to it, but it was this moment I began to be free of my pain and to see the world more as God sees it: through God's eyes, or more precisely, through love.

I finally had the answer for that question from so many decades below on the busy Wyoming interstate. The answer to "what is love?" is that "God is love" (I Jn 4:8). Love is neither action nor feeling. Instead, both actions and feelings are like the pause associated with a comma; they are the result rather than the definition of love. Love is the lens through which we view the world, and in order to truly be able to love others free of expectations or selfishness, we must see the world through the filter of God's "love, joy, peace, patience, kindness, goodness, faithfulness, gentleness, [and] self-control" (Gal 5:22-23a).

Seeking God

One of the trickiest situations I have to handle as an English teacher isn't behavior management or parent communications—though those are high on the list—but is, instead, the task of getting students to write for me. Nearly every student, about 90% of the ones I have personally worked with, is afraid of failing—especially when it comes to papers. Writing with the knowledge that the person who will be evaluating or "judging" their work and will likely catch all of the errors seems horribly intimidating to pretty much any teenager I've ever taught. They want to write perfectly the first time, but they know they can't, so they refuse. Students, much like many of us as adults, have made *perfect* the enemy of *good*.

In similar ways, putting God on the throne sounds hard because we think that before we can do that, we have to clean out what's there, but that's not true. There's a part of us that continues to make *perfect* the enemy of the *good* just as my students are prone to do. We can't do it all the way immediately, so we don't even try. But the throne of our hearts is filled with what we want to be there whether it is God or money or something else entirely. While it may be difficult at first, as soon as we decide we want to put God there, we're on the right track. He tells us constantly that if we seek Him, He will be there for us.

"But from there you will seek the Lord your God and you will find Him, if you search after Him with all your heart and with all your soul" (Dt 4:29).

"I love those who love me, and those who seek me diligently find me" (Pr. 8:17).

However, the promises don't just stop there. God isn't a father who ignores His children for better things to do. He doesn't just say that if we look for Him, we'll find Him like a small child who finds his father working hard but unavailable. Instead, these promises are that He is there and has great things for us if we just seek Him. If we truly want to see God, all we have to do is look for Him. And when we find Him, He's available for us.

"But seek first the kingdom of God and his righteousness, and all these things will be added to you" (Mt 6:33).

"Seek the Lord while He may be found; call upon Him while He is near" (Is 55:6).

"But those who seek the Lord lack no good thing" (Ps 34:10b).

"Ask, and it will be given to you; seek, and you will find; knock, and it will be opened to you. For everyone who asks receives, and the one who seeks finds, and to the one who knocks it will be opened" (Mt 7:7-8).

"And without faith it is impossible to please him, for whoever would draw near to God must believe that he exists and that he rewards those who seek him" (Heb 11:6).

But be aware, there's a warning too. God is not limited to our view of love. Later, I will address love and justice, but I don't want to introduce this idea of seeking a loving Father only to create a misunderstanding. God is still a God of justice and righteousness. As you can see in the Scripture below, Hosea warns that there is a time for seeking the Lord, and, the presumed antithesis to such a statement, is that there could be a time when it's too late to seek God's will for us and our lives.

"Sow for yourselves righteousness; reap steadfast love; break up your fallow ground, for it is the time to seek the Lord, that He may come and rain righteousness upon you." (Hos 10:12)

We know we live in a finite world where life begins and ends according to time. We are limited by this restraint, and we must be aware that there does come a point of no return. If we are not reaping love (or sowing it for that matter), we run a risk of losing our chance to do so. And the way we sow and reap love can be best done by seeking the Lord. But never forget that after Pharaoh hardened his own heart five times, God removed the choice from him when it says, "But the Lord hardened the heart of Pharaoh" (Ex 9:12). From that point on, Pharaoh was incapable of recanting his stance; he had lost his chance to sow or reap love. At some point, if we continue to harden our own hearts and ignore the voice of the Lord, we could reach the point of no return as well.

With all of that being said, how do we seek God? Is it a simple prayer that you give like a child asking God to enter your heart? Is it a routine reading and memorization of the Scriptures? Does it mean ridding yourself of all your mental "junk food" (i.e., unnecessary television, books, etc.)? What does it look like to seek God?

One lesson I've learned is that seeking God looks very different on every different person. For one, seeking God may be seeking opportunities to help others. For another, seeking God means studying His Word and hiding it in their hearts. And again, others may seek God by pursuing a career that directly influences the expansion of God's kingdom—e.g., missionaries, Bible translators, etc. In whatever way we choose to seek God out in our lives, however, one thing remains the same: our faith needs to be centered on His Word so that we can fight the storms of this world. I often think of it as if I am Columbus sailing into unknown waters. I know that I have to have a direction to head, but I have no clue what I might hit on the way. Each day, when we wake up, we must check our direction and make sure we are still following Christ. After our focus is set, we can learn to see the world through the lens of God's love no matter what storms come our way.

A year or two before that infamous car ride that started my quest to define love, we were living in a log cabin in the countryside outside of Colville in Washington state. The cabin had no electricity and no running water. The downstairs consisted of one large room with the kitchen taking up two walls in one corner, and the rest was open. Upstairs, a loft sporting a wooden railing covered half the downstairs and overlooked the rest facing large windows open to the outside of one side of the cabin. It was perhaps one of the coolest places to live when you're a child. The snow banks we regularly experienced throughout the two very cold winters would pile up above our heads (admittedly we were not much more than two and half feet tall); what child wouldn't love that? But, it is also the location of much of the abuse and suffering I experienced as a child.

That abuse eventually resulted in a call to Child Protective Services, and for a day, my brother and I were removed from the home and placed with a foster family. My mother, who didn't know the full extent of what we were being subjected to, was able to put a stop to it and brought us home. I was being brought up in the church by a mother who loved Christ, but this foster parent who I had for one night put my suffering into the perspective of God's love with her kind actions and timely, Christ-like words. Dating my conversion to Christianity is hard because He has always mattered to me, but if I had to pinpoint it, it would be in those two days.

Due to age, emotional trauma, and physical trauma (during this time, I had an exceptionally bad bout of strep throat that caused a 106° fever), I don't remember a lot of details—only the major life events stuck with me with a few flashes of others. As time has removed me from then, more and more makes its way back into my conscious memories. Perhaps one of the most powerful memories was from one of my mother's Bible lessons.

She was teaching us the sermon on the mount. While my mother wasn't great about teaching us the traditional Sunday School Bible stories, she was very good at teaching us deeper concepts of faith and laying a foundation of theology that we would reference over our entire lives. This particular lesson took place shortly after the events described above. I don't remember much from it other than the Scripture and the thought that filled my head: "Blessed are those who hunger and thirst for righteousness for they shall be satisfied." (Mt 5:6) and all I could think to ask was "Lord, please don't let me be satisfied. I always want to hunger and thirst for you!" As I grew in understanding, I realized that my wish wasn't directly correlated to what the Scripture was saying in that moment, but the wish followed me for a few years. And then, as they say, life happened, as it so often does for us in our time-limited world, until even the memory of that wish faded with time. As an adult, I've had times where I have tried to seek the Lord, but I felt lost in my attempts, as if I was traveling through a city trying to get to the other side without a road map. My own hurt and bitterness prevented me from seeing the road map that was right in front of me.

But in the last few years, with the release of my bitterness, that road map has become clear again. My childhood wish was refreshed, and I can look back and see the amazing work of God in my life—even in the suffering. A part of me feels ashamed that I hadn't found it before, but another part of me is more grateful that I have received it back. The truth is, that road map has been prayer. Not the little prayers of children or the long-winded prayers of the "theologically sound." But rather, my own prayers inspired by Scripture. My prayers are not always what I want them to be, but I can see my growth when I allow myself to talk to God rather than to view Him as a supreme being far beyond my reach. Perhaps one of the greatest assists I received in this area came from the book *Moving Mountains* by John Eldridge—an exploration of prayer and the different uses of prayers. I especially loved his chapter on "The Call of the Heart." So many things have happened since that day in Wyoming, but the most impactful was finding a clear definition of love and learning how to apply that to my life.

Loving Our Neighbors through the Lens of Loving God

On that note, now is a good time to turn to the topic of this chapter: loving our neighbors. Christ summed up the law and the prophets in what we now refer to as the two great commandments:

> "You shall love the Lord your God with all your heart and with all your soul and with all your mind...You shall love your neighbor as yourself." (Mt 22:37, 39)

The truth is, it is impossible to fulfill the second command without fulfilling the first. In seeking God first, people can begin to see others as He sees them. Those around us who have hurt us become, in our eyes, lost sheep who need the shepherd. Those who would break us become the broken who need help. As C.S. Lewis points out in *Mere Christianity*, we see only the results which a man's choices make out of his raw material. We don't get to see his raw material. When we look at people through the love of God, we see that they are fighting battles beyond our own imagination.

As we begin to view people as being made up of parts so much deeper than we see, we realize that we can, in fact, love those who hurt us. Because God is on the throne in our hearts, we see others through the lens of His word. God's instruction, His teachings, which are given to us in both the Old and New Testaments of His holy Word become our guideposts. While we are not perfect, and we mess up all the time, each day we can move closer to our goal of loving God with all that we are and begin to love others in the ways which were commanded.

But, we should never become complacent in such an important and monumental task. We should always be engaged in self-examination to make sure we are measuring up to our greatest potential. In order to examine ourselves, we can always reference the words of Paul to the church at Corinth:

> "Love is patient and kind; love does not envy or boast; it is not arrogant or rude. It does not insist on its own way; it is not irritable or resentful; it does not rejoice at wrongdoing, but boasts all things, believes all things, hopes all things, endures all things. Love never ends … So now faith, hope, and love abide, these three; but the greatest of these is love." (I Cor 13:4-8, 13)

So, how do we love our neighbors? We take a deep breath and we pray every day. We ask for God's vision to be our vision and for the ability to look at the world through the lens of what He has done for us. We pray for the salvation of every soul on Earth, both those we know and those we don't. Don't forget the story of Corrie Ten Boom, the woman who helped so many Jews hide and survive the Holocaust. After her release from prison, when she was unexpectedly confronted by one of her jailers from that traumatic past, she described that experience by admitting that she "wrestled with the most difficult thing I had ever had to do. For I had to do it — I knew that. The message that God forgives has a prior condition: that we forgive those who have injured us." Neither love nor forgiveness are easy, and they do not come from us; they come from God. Later, I will discuss the relationship between love and forgiveness more in depth, but for now, I will say that when we struggle to love or to forgive, our only option is to go to God.

What about those who actively despise us? How do we handle that? I know that for me personally, it has been a true struggle. Much like many others, I have at times failed in this particular arena.

For a year, I worked in southern China, near Hong Kong, in one of their largest cities, Shenzhen. I was a literature teacher at a private school. It was an amazing year for experiences, but one of my most spiritually dry seasons. I had no one around me who even claimed Christianity and no church I could visit. While I did have access to my Bible both physically and electronically, I found that I never read it. At the same time, a tension built up between me and my department head—so strong in fact that it was known to all of the school. Her dislike of me as well as my dislike for her colored the entire department. Even students knew, and those students who liked her disliked me and the ones who liked me disliked her. It was a horrible sinful grudge I held against her, and even now, I regret it. In this place, I failed to show the Christian love I was called to show to her, and the result was damage to the name of Christ. I left the school feeling ashamed of myself and my own behavior.

I understand how hard it is to show love, but that failure was what has pushed me to, even now, seek God first. I thought then that I knew what was commanded of me, and I could do it, but on my own, I failed. Since then, life has moved forward, and God has led me down many different paths. I am writing this in the hopes of helping to prevent others from suffering the same kind of failures or to recover from past mistakes already committed. As so many before, this experience taught me that I am incapable of doing the right thing on my own.

How do we keep from falling into that place of hating or despising someone else? The only answer I have found is to take our eyes off man and put them on God. Seeking God first will allow all of the other things to fall into place, and it will shield us from falling into *that* place of resentment or bitterness. And seeking God is most easily accomplished through regular prayer.

On the other hand, David, who is described as being a man after God's own heart, had many enemies. Perhaps the longest ongoing trial was the conflict with Saul, the king of Israel before David took the throne. On several occasions Saul attempted to kill the young man, but when given the opportunity to rid himself of the danger to his own life, David chose to trust God and leave judgment of Saul to the greatest judge. While Saul relieved himself in the cave where David was hiding, David spared his life because he was God's anointed king (I Sam 24).

When we read the Psalms, we see David's heart cry out to God over and over again begging for justice, but David also knew that justice comes from God, and not from man. Does that mean we as a nation should give over our homes to every unjust person and wait for God to smite them to the ground? No, we are called to be righteous and to protect others from injustice such as in Isaiah where we are told to "learn to do good; seek justice; correct oppression" (1:17a). But it does mean that we are not to seek vengeance for ourselves because "vengeance is mine ... says the Lord" (Ro 12:19 qt. Dt 32:35).

Rather than looking for slights and insults, we are to look for those who have suffered greatly. We are supposed to be like the Samaritan who helped that man beaten and robbed on the road. As we go through life, we should look for chances to reach out to others and to help them.

There's a set of books that I read about Jewish culture at the time of Christ that I fondly think of as the "Rabbi Jesus" books—*Sitting at the Feet of Rabbi Jesus, Walking in the Dust of Rabbi Jesus,* and *Reading the Bible with Rabbi Jesus.* They completely changed my understanding of various aspects of Jewish life and even clarified the meanings of some of the words of Christ and Paul that I hadn't understood prior to reading them.

But perhaps one of the most meaningful aspects of the books is it allowed me to understand how Jews view the world around them. A touching part to me, which I later discuss in much more detail, was the description of how Jews actively seek out ways to "love" their neighbors as they're commanded to do in Deuteronomy. They believe, and I have come to believe it as well, that God has set up their paths to be filled with small, and sometimes large, ways they can show love to others throughout the day. It's kind of like a game—can we find how God has set up this day for me to show love to someone else? Imagine what life would be like if we all walked around every day asking that question and looking for opportunities to help others.

Love, as so many concepts, is not an easy one to break apart mostly because we often don't take the time to consider the implications. But the truth is, love from a Christian perspective isn't too hard to understand. It is simply seeing the world and everyone and everything in it through the lens of the Lord and Christ our Savior. True love puts God first and then serves others. Seeing the world through that lens only comes from seeking Him every day of our life. And truly seeking Him results in actions that are loving to our neighbors. But this is really only the beginning of the conversation about biblical love.

2

LOVE AND GRACE

Grace: The Free Gift

As a person who has been raised in the Christian community, I have often been taught that it is by the grace of God that we have been saved. His grace is what leads to our justification, salvation, and glorification. When I was a child, the simple definition of grace was that it is the thing God gave us that we didn't deserve it. Honestly, I struggled with that idea of grace because it seemed ... lackluster. Wasn't grace supposed to be this amazing thing that would change how we saw the world and how we lived our lives? An undeserved gift is like a present on your birthday that you're given because you were born. It just didn't seem so great. And even beyond that, what was it a gift of? Sure, it's something we've received, but what did we receive?

The first time that the Scriptures mention the grace of God is in Proverbs. There, Solomon tells us that "toward the scorners [the Lord] is scornful, but to the humble he gives [grace]"[1] (Prov 3:34). What does that mean for us now? Is grace earned through humility? And, if it's earned through humility, is it truly the free gift of God? Do we receive more grace if we are *more* humble?

My best answer for this is that "the law was given through Moses; grace and truth came through Jesus Christ" (Jn 1:17). The law given by Moses teaches us what is right and wrong—even making allowances for our sinful and imperfect natures—but Christ's "law" shows us that it's only by the favor shown to us by God that we can be justified. If we should actually follow the law of Christ rather than His grace, we would fail miserably because Christ requires us to maintain complete control of our thoughts as well as our actions (Mt 5:21-30).

Is grace a "free" gift, an "undeserved" gift, or is it something else entirely? Paul said it very nicely in his letter to the church at Rome when he said:

"But the free gift is not like the trespass [the sin of Adam]. For if many died through one man's trespass, much more have the grace of God and the free gift by the grace of that one man Jesus Christ abounded for many." (Rom 5:15)

"Free gift" is, in a sense, an accurate definition; we're just left not clearly understanding what that gift was: eternal life, love, favor, all of the above, or something else entirely. It's summed up best saying that the grace of God was the free gift of the sacrifice of the Son as atonement for our sin which would then include all of the other benefits such as eternal life, God's favor, and His love. It is the outworking of God's love. Remember how we often define love as either *action* or *feeling* … well, grace is the correct term to use for the actions of love. The free gift we've been given isn't justification, sanctification, or glorification; it is the love of God for "greater love has no one than this, that someone lay down his life for his friends" (Jn 15:13). While I cannot presume to know what is in the heart of God, I do know that He looks at us through the lens of His love for us, and the free gift of love is the only reason He would have sent His Son to die for our sins.

God's Love for Us

Because grace is the outworking of God's love, what I really want to explore here is God's love for us. The most obvious example of this has to do with the sacrifice of Christ: "for God so loved the world that he gave his one and only son so that whoever believes in Him will not perish, but will have everlasting life" (Jn 3:16). The beauty of this passage sometimes becomes lost on us because we've heard it so much, but this is a perfect picture of God's grace because it is the action born out of His love for us.

If we consider the depth to God's love for us, we can go back to the very beginning when God made Adam and declared His creation "good" (Gen 1:31). Adam was neither a Jew nor a Gentile, but instead, was just a man. God created him and loved him just as He created Eve and loved her. In the beginning, we were a creation that was declared as 'good' by the God of the universe.

I am an amateur artist. I create various pieces just for the enjoyment of the act, and I use various mediums from pencil to paint to needle and thread. As an artist, I can tell you there is a special feeling between creator and creation, and I'm certain that God feels this way about His creation—about us. What some may even consider a "mar" or "mistake" can often create something so much more beautiful than if it had been perfectly executed because it made the creation that much more unique, exquisite, and irreplaceable.

God is creating in us something so much more beautiful than anything we could have imagined. And, He declares His love for all of those who seek Him regardless of their sins and shortcomings—even as far back as the creation of the tablets of His law when He proclaimed to Moses that He is "The Lord, the Lord, a God merciful and gracious, slow to anger, and abounding in steadfast love and faithfulness, keeping steadfast love for thousands, forgiving iniquity and transgression and sin" (Ex 34:6-7a). God's grace isn't limited to those of us born after He came to earth for us; instead, it is there for all who love Him from the dawn of time to now and until His return.

Over and over again, the Bible tells of the steadfast love of God from the time of Moses to the time of Paul.

"The Lord is slow to anger and abounding in steadfast love forgiving iniquity and transgression" (Nu 14:18a).

"The Lord your God will keep with you the covenant and the steadfast love that he swore to your fathers" (Deut 7:12b).

"Because the Lord loved Israel forever, he has made you king that you may execute justice and righteousness" (I Kings 10:9b).

"But you are a God ready to forgive, gracious and merciful, slow to anger and abounding in steadfast love, and did not forsake them" (Neh 9:17b).

"Now, therefore, our God, the great, the mighty, and the awesome God, who keeps covenant and steadfast love" (Neh 9:32a).

There are so many more in Psalms, Proverbs, and the Prophets that I can't list them all here, but these few show us all that God has had a great love for all of us since the beginning of time. Considering that God is a God of truth, then this love will continue to work its way into our lives by the means of grace; that is, by means of the free gift of His Son who was sent because He sees us through His own love for us.

Now the love spoken of in the old testament, for a time, specifically addresses (but is not necessarily limited to) the Israelites. Why was that the case? We may never know fully while we are on this Earth, but it was through them that He brought about salvation for all. Those descendants of Abraham are a truly blessed people.

(As a side note, I will say that I find myself praying constantly in hope of the redemption and salvation of the Israelites. It was through Israel that God showed His true love for us so that we will "have come to know and to believe the love that God has for us." (I Jn 4:16a). God's people have a special covenant with Him, and I personally would like to see it renewed.)

Back to the topic of God's grace which is the outpouring of His love for us, we see that God's love for us is more than just sending His Son to die for our sins as an atoning sacrifice. God, much like our fathers and mothers today, loves us enough to spend time teaching us what is right and wrong.

While it is true that modern Rabbinic Judaism denies Christ, there is still much we can learn from traditional Judaism. Perhaps one of the strongest effects of learning about Jewish culture and beliefs for me was a simple turn of phrase. All of my life, I have been taught that Moses was given the law of God and that Jesus was the fulfillment of that law. However, Jews do not think of what Moses was given as "law" but rather as a "teaching." The very word that we translate as *law* is, for as long back as we can track, more accurately translated as *teaching* in the context of the Bible. It is God teaching us right and wrong.

With this simple switch of thinking, it completely changed how I understood the entire Bible, but especially the first five books; however, it wasn't limited just to those five books, it also included passages in Psalms, Proverbs, and even some of the words of Christ. I no longer saw the God of the Old Testament as a harsh taskmaster giving a law. In His wisdom, He took the time to teach us the basics of good and evil before teaching us the nuances of the law. He told us it was wrong to murder (Ex 20:13) before He told us it was wrong to wish someone dead (Mt 5:21-22). Slowly, I began to see Him as a father who was trying to prepare us for a battle, to show us what we would need so that we would have a goal to reach for and a true victory over death and sin.

While I am not as much of an individualist as my sister is, I don't like being told what to do any more than the next person. However, there is Psalm after Psalm talking about how great the law is and what a joy it is to think about. For instance, Psalm 119:48. But, after considering the difference between "law" and "teaching" it took on a whole different level of connection for me where the Psalmist declares, "I will lift up my hands toward your commandments, which I love, and I will meditate on your statutes." This isn't really talking about loving rules and commands given by an invisible God, but instead, it's talking about loving the teaching of a personal God.

Consider this earlier Scripture and think about it in terms of this change in vocabulary. In Deuteronomy 7:12-13, Moses, communicating from God, tells the people:

> "And because you listen to these rules and keep and do them, the Lord your God will keep with you the covenant and the steadfast love that He swore to your fathers. He will love you, bless you, and multiply you. He will also bless the fruit of your womb and the fruit of your ground, your grain and your wine and your oil, the increase of your herds and the young of your flock, in the land that He swore to your fathers to give you."

Note here that God is making a promise of steadfast love that comes with what appears to be stipulations of obedience to His law. If a father said this to his children, anyone who heard this would be, at the very least, indignant. But let's change the tone a little bit by changing one single word. Replace "rules" with "instructions." Following instructions is not the same as following rules as we understand that instructions can be messed up and then corrected whereas a broken rule, once broken, is always broken. It's easier to fix a messed-up instruction than to fix a broken rule. Also, instructions teach us how to make something work whereas rules set limitations. Perhaps here, God is telling His people how to make things work in our world rather than setting arbitrary limitations.

We can be certain that God's love has no stipulations because "God shows his love for us in that while we were still sinners, Christ died for us" (Rom 5:8). However, love and blessings aren't the same thing. We should always be aware that while nothing can separate us from the love of God (Rom 8:38-39), Christ did not come to abolish the law (Mt 5:17)—or, more precisely, to abolish the teaching of the Old Testament. God's love for us is immeasurable (Eph 3:18), and that means that He wants what is best for us.

We, like children, can only see that which is right in front of our eyes at any given moment. God, our good and loving Father, knows more than we are capable of even imagining. As children, if we learn to follow the instructions given to us by our parents, then we learn how to interact and succeed in life. It's the same with our relationship with God. If we listen to His instructions and trust that He wants what is best for us, we may find that everything will work together for our good (Ro 8:28).

Common Grace

Common grace is a term that I've heard used to describe how God treats the unbeliever. As Matthew records, Jesus said that "He makes His sun rise on the evil and the good, and sends rain on the just and on the unjust" (5:45). For thousands of years, God has preserved mankind, both good and evil. We ourselves do not know who in our ancestry was saved by miraculous works, but we know that our entire family lines were preserved through this idea of common grace.

As the years have passed, I find myself no longer believing that there is a common grace for unbelievers and a special grace for believers. Instead, I think of my own family line, and I realize that all grace is the love of God sent for those who believe in Him. He knew us before the dawn of time (Jer 1:5; Ps 139:16; Rom 8:29; Eph 1:4), and He works everything together for the good of those who love Him (Rom 8:28).

Imagine, for a moment if you will, a hot summer day in the savannas of Africa maybe 1,000 years ago. A little girl watches as the wind blows through the trees some distance away. The dry grass is so brittle that it doesn't even bend in the wind. Instead the few bristles still standing, now stand tall against the heavy breeze while most of the grass has withered into almost nothingness. It had been so long since the last rain, her parents were worried about how they were going to have enough of a harvest to feed themselves and their five children over the next year. So worried, in fact, that they had more than once visited the shaman priests of their tribe who lived several miles away. But this day was a bit different, and the strong wind carried with it the scent of hope, the scent of rain. Today, she wasn't watching a blazing sun in a sapphire sky, but instead, in the not very far distance, she could see the darkness that had been gathering come towards them. The sun was disappearing behind the clouds coming from the western skies, and with the clouds came the promise of rain. Sure enough, not more than ten minutes later came the first drops of what promised to be just the remedy for the scorched fields and crops.

Now, imagine for a moment, that child is your ancestor or my ancestor or the ancestor of your spouse or best friend or pastor. Was that just "common" grace, or was it the love of God who knew us before the dawn of time and preserved our family lines so that all things would work together for our good? This may have happened in order for either you or me to be here today, and the people today who seem to prosper under this "common grace" of the world but live horrible lives may one day be the ancestor of another believer who we will be in close communion with in eternity.

Let me give you an example of this kind of "common grace" in my own life that may not seem so gracious, but has actually been a great outpouring of God's love. I remember when I was about four years old, the summer of 1990, we were in a major transition in our lives. But on this particularly hot June day, I found myself being dressed in the bathroom of a motel room in clothes that were fancier than most of my wardrobe at the time. Not too long before this, we had lost our home because it had been ruined from the smoke damage of a kitchen fire, and we had lost almost every possession we had at the time. But this day, we were dressed up and taken to a building that looked like a church, but it wasn't. This place wasn't about joy and blessing. This was something different entirely. People didn't go to this building to worship God. The seats were wooden benches with red cushions, and we sat in the front row. At the front of the room was a large, shiny wooden box. I was still too small to see inside the box, but when the talking was done, we all walked up there with my mother. She took turns lifting my brother and me to see inside—everyone else was tall enough to see inside on their own—and what I saw appeared to be a doll that looked just like my father. In all actuality, it was the first dead body I had ever seen. It's probably the only thing I can clearly remember from that summer, but the image is seared into my mind.

How could such an event be the outpouring of God's love? Well, not too long after that June day in Houston, my mother took all of us and moved to Oregon. Events were set into motion that resulted in my mother meeting and marrying a man who would become my stepfather. Now, this sounds like it might have a fairy-tale ending, but it didn't. That man was not a good man, but it took some time before that was known. During the interim, my mother became pregnant and gave birth, not once, but twice. Had my father lived, or my mother made a wiser choice about her next husband, these two people wouldn't exist now. For as hard as my life was, I am more convinced now than I have ever been that all things work together for the good of those who love God because while I was still a sinner, God loved me (Rom 5:8).

We, as Christians, are also a bit of common grace that God sends into the world for those who are unbelievers. We can do things for others, help them, because we know what real love is—real love is seeing everyone through the lens of God's love for us. Once we see the world that way, it's easier for us to give people the benefit of the doubt, to help them when they're in need, and to seek God's will first for all of those around us. When Jesus taught us to pray, He taught us to ask for God's "will be done on earth as it is in heaven" (Mt 5:10b). When we look at the world through God's love and grace for all of those that are His, *and* we fully trust that all things are being controled by God, it becomes much easier to pray for His will over our own.

God has planted various seeds of grace throughout this world, whether it be sunshine and rain, or those who love Him. As a people we should remember that we are trees planted by God and given life by the blood of Christ, and a "tree is known by its fruit" (Mt 12:33b). We should love others not because it's our duty, but because it's our privilege. Love and grace come from God, and we are privileged to share in its abundance, so we should also share that abundance with others. So, I will reiterate: we are, at least in part, the common grace of God.

Grace and Works

Some years ago, I remember talking to my baby sister who was, at that time, barely 12 years old. She had become very attached to the book of James, and I couldn't understand what attracted a 12-year-old to a book that is so often used to justify the theology of a works-based salvation. More recently, though, as my thought patterns and perceptions began to change, and I began to see God's words as teachings and not laws, I could see what she saw back then.

James tells us very clearly that "faith by itself, if it does not have works, is dead" (2:17). That has a lasting implication for us, who are under grace and saved by faith. That doesn't mean that the free gift of God's love actually isn't free. However, it does mean that we should constantly be examining ourselves, our actions, and our motives. If we are experiencing God's love at any given time, it will be visible in our actions each day.

If we claim to be under grace and looking at the world through the lens of God's love, but we see all these people who need help, and we know the right thing to do, but we don't do it, are we truly looking through the lens of love? If Christ lives in our heart (Gal 2:20), and Christ is God (Jn 8:58), and God is love (I Jn 4:8), but we don't love others, what right do we have to claim salvation? Doing good is not the cause of our salvation any more than a pause is the cause of a comma; rather, doing good is the outcome of our salvation. Our desire to help others and to love our neighbors comes from the love of God being on the throne in our hearts.

James goes on to tell us that "Someone will say, 'You have faith and I have works. Show me your faith apart from your works, and *I will show you my faith by my works.*" (2:18). We are not called to salvation by the works of our hands, but rather, we are called to use our works as a demonstration of our faith.

Perhaps the best example of this to me is the story of Brother Andrew in *God's Smuggler*. That book tells the real story of a man who, for the very love of his fellow man, risked life and limb to supply Christians in countries behind the iron curtain (communist countries in the mid-20th century) with the Word of God. He didn't do that work so that he would be saved; he did that work because he was saved. He loved his fellow man with a love that could only come as a demonstration of his own salvation. Reading that story was, for me, a revelation in what it means to truly have God sitting on the throne in our hearts.

Paul, when writing to the church at Colossae, tells us that "whatever [we] do, work heartily, as for the Lord and not for men knowing that from the Lord you will receive the inheritance as your reward" (3:23-24a). We should always be working for God, and not for men. Our works are incapable of saving us "for all have sinned and fall short of the glory of God" (Rom 3:23), but they are the outworking of our faith. Our faith, much as James describes Abraham's faith is "completed by [our] works" (2:22b).

So that we don't lose sight of the main topic, let me end with this note. Works are an outpouring of our faith just as grace is the outpouring of God's love for us. What we do *cannot* save us, but what we do *does* demonstrate whether or not we've been saved: "For by grace you have been saved through faith. And this not of your own doing; it is the gift of God, not a result of works, so that no one may boast" (Eph 2:8-9) but "faith without works is dead" (James 2:17). We will be recognized by our own fruits just as we will "recognize them by their fruits" (Mt 7:16).

3

LOVE AND HOPE

Hope

Hope is a word layered with meanings. As our children apply for colleges, they express their *hope* that they will get into the college that they wish. This is a deep yearning or desire for something. When we say things like "I hope it will rain soon," we're expressing a *desire* or a *want* for rain, not so much a heart-wrenching yearning from deep within our soul. There's nothing wrong with desiring these things, of course. For thousands of years, rain has been a major desire because water gives us life. Which college we go to can have a lasting impact on our lives as well. But, when we say our hope is in God, I know I am referring to that yearning that comes out of the deepest part of myself, and that is very different from just a desire or want.

When doing some research for this book, I found some very interesting tidbits of information about the words translated as "hope." The words are also translated as "wait" and "trust." So, when the Psalmist says, "Let your steadfast love, O Lord, be upon us, even as we hope in you" (33:22), he is also saying, "even as we wait on you" or "even as we trust in you."

Hoping in the Lord requires much more from us than just a desire for Him. A desire for the promises of the Lord without trust or patience can be a dangerous motivator for us to take drastic actions. Consider this: I have heard it argued, though I don't know if there is any truth to it, that Judas Iscariot's betrayal of Christ was done in the *hopes* of spurring Him into action as the military leader that many Jews *hoped* the Messiah would be. Such a conviction and hope is more than a little detrimental and can lead us to do things that we would normally find abhorrent.

That being said, what is it to put our "hope in Christ" (Eph 1:12) and to "trust in him" (Heb 2:12)? As hard as this answer can be to accept and to apply, isn't the right answer to:

"Wait for the Lord; be strong, and let your heart take courage; wait for the Lord!" (Ps 27:14)

"Be still and know that I am God" (Ps 46:10a).

"He who has an ear, let him hear what the Spirit says" (Rev 2:7, 11, 17, 29; 3:6, 13, 22).

Remembering that God speaks using a "still small voice" (I Kings 19:12), we should make it a habit to sit quietly and meditate on his teaching both day and night. We can model this after how the Psalmist described the blessed man when he said, "but his delight is in the law of the Lord, and on his law he meditates day and night" (Ps 1:2). When I read this verse, I like to remind myself that the word for "law" is the same word used for "instruction" or "teaching," it makes the verse much more meaningful to me.

Hope and Faith

Before we can get further into listening for God, waiting on His will, and trusting fully in Him, we have to explore the foundation of our hope: faith. Faith, much like hope, is a word layered in meanings, but I think it's best defined as "the assurance of things hoped for, the conviction of things not seen" (Heb 11:1).

Faith being described as the belief in things unseen always makes me go back to "doubting" Thomas. A part of me feels bad that this is the story we all know about this man when, doubtless, there were a great many wonderful events surrounding him as well as examples of his faith, but I think that this man's momentary doubt was given to us so that we could hear Jesus say, "Blessed are those who have not seen and yet have believed." This is an encouragement for us who did not see Christ in the flesh, but rather believe that He did in fact appear in the flesh and was resurrected in the flesh after paying the full price for our sins.

Faith is something all people have—even if it's not in God. But, to build on our earlier metaphor of a throne in our hearts, imagine a tree of faith growing out of that throne with the roots nourished by whatever it is we hold dearest. If it's Christ who dominates our hearts, then the faith that we are growing will be fed by our hope and belief in Him, but if it's something else such as Science or the General Goodness of Mankind, then our faith is reassigned to those areas.

Being an English teacher, I have taught many poems over the years, but none touched me in quite the same way as Emily Dickinson's short "Hope is a Thing with Feathers" verse did. Here, she compares hope to a small bird perched in the soul that can withstand harsh weather and drought. This bird never asks for even a crumb, but just sits there providing its song to any who would stop to listen. It's a beautiful sentiment, but hope, without a tree to perch on, will fly away.

We need faith in order to have hope. Without faith, there is nowhere for our bird of hope to perch, and the result of no faith is that the bird will fly away not even leaving behind a single feather. But, as Peter instructed us, we should be "preparing [our] minds for action, and being sober-minded, set [our] hope fully on the grace that will be brought to [us] at the revelation of Jesus Christ" (I Pet 1:13). If our hope is founded on the grace and love of Christ who died for us and was resurrected, then we are preparing ourselves for the return of Christ.

Hope for the Hopeless

If "God is love" (I Jn 4:8), and Christ is God (Jn 8:58), and faith comes from "hearing the Word of Christ" (Ro 10:17), and faith is the assurance of hope (Heb 11:1), then it follows that hope is the result of God's love for us.

We hope because we have the assurance that there is something to be hoped for. Obviously, at times, we still struggle to maintain that hope, but even then, in our heads, we understand what we're hoping for. During those struggles when we want to find our way back, all we have to do is stop and listen for the still small voice of the bird chirping in the distance; we can find our way back because God is always there waiting for us.

Perhaps one of the most beautiful examples of this is the story of Naomi. While Ruth is one of the most romantic stories of the Bible, Naomi's is one of great suffering. She lost her husband and her sons and went back to her home country to die. She considered herself cursed and at the receiving end of God's hand of judgment (Ru 1:13). Naomi experienced some of the deepest levels of depression during this time, and I'm sure she saw no way out of the situation. Here she was, a childless widow with no grandchildren and two widowed daughters-in-law from a foreign land. She knew that if her daughters followed her home, they would almost certainly be left widowed and childless, so she tried to spare them from her own fate. There's no way she could have known what was coming—that she was going to be the great-great-grandmother of the greatest king of Israel, David, and, eventually, Naomi's line, through Ruth and Boaz, would include the Eternal King, Christ Himself. Obviously, she couldn't have known, but even in her depression, she still sought out God's will.

By the end of the story, the women of Bethlehem declared to Naomi, "Blessed be the Lord, who has not left you this day without a redeemer and may his name be renowned in Israel! He shall be to you a restorer of life and a nourisher of your old age, for your daughter-in-law who loves you, who is more to you than seven sons, has given birth to him" (Ru 4:14-15). We ourselves have a kinsman redeemer who has sacrificed Himself for us (Is 60:16). We can declare with Job that "I know that my

Redeemer lives, and at the last he will stand upon the earth" (Job 19:25).

Job was also one of the very tragic stories of the Bible. He, for reasons only partially shared with us, suffers greatly at the hands of the Devil. He loses his home, his possessions, his children, his wife, and even his own health, but not because of anything that he has done. His friends tell him that he must have committed some great sin; his wife condemns him and tells him to turn his back on God. But Job somehow manages to hold on fast to his faith. He rebuffs the accusations of his friends, and doesn't give in to the demand of his wife. Eventually, though, even he begins to question God. The response was, well, biblical in proportions, and Job repented with these words:

> "Therefore I have uttered what I did not understand, things too wonderful for me, which I did not know ... I had heard of you by the hearing of the ear, but now my eye sees you; therefore I despise myself, and repent in dust and ashes" (Job 42:3, 5-6).

Job knew, even at this point, that his hope, for this life and the next, only existed within the very grace of God.

I have been down the dark path of depression, and it seemed to me so often that I couldn't find a way out of that pit they call despair. As so many others, I had been advised to look to the promises of God, consider all of these people who suffered, or even to repent of my despair because it's a sin, but none of that seemed to work. This very book is born out of what brought me out of my own despair, and it wasn't anything that I personally did. I didn't change my perspective or look at things differently. What brought me out of my own despair was the very love and grace of God. It was the renewing of my faith in "the assurance of things hoped for and the conviction of things not seen" (Heb 11:1).

What we Hope for

So, what do we hope for? Matthew, referencing Isaiah, says of Jesus that "in his name the Gentiles will hope" (Mt 12:21). We hope in the name of Christ. We trust in Christ. We wait on Christ. Because to hope for something is to trust that it will happen, to want it to happen, and to wait on it to happen.

As Paul so clearly outlined for us, we hope in the glory of God because God has spent precious time building in us the character of one who can hope:

> "Therefore, since we have been justified by faith, we have peace with God through our Lord Jesus Christ. Through him we have also obtained access by faith into the grace in which we stand, and we rejoice in hope of the glory of God. Not only that, but we rejoice in our sufferings, knowing that suffering produces endurance, and endurance produces character, and character produces hope, and hope does not put us to shame, because God's love has been poured into our hearts through the Holy Spirit who has been given to us" (Ro 5:1-5).

Our sufferings are not a punishment, curse, or plague sent to remind us who God is, or anything so spiteful as that seems to be. Our sufferings are the very events in our lives that allow us to become the kind of people who can hope in God. If we never have to ask for help, how can we appreciate the beauty of the experience of being helped? In *God's Smuggler*, the wonderful account of Brother Andrew's life spent working for the expansion of God's kingdom that I mentioned in the last chapter, he is constantly experiencing the help I'm speaking about. He has no problem asking for help and watching as God provides it with the same wide eyes as a child watching his father who, with a few quick motions, fixes a seemingly unfixable toy.

If we hope for the glory of God, then we have the assurance that, not only is it real, but that we will get to experience it one day. We hope for that which is coming, and we look to Christ in the hopes of seeing Him and being a part of His glory. Christ even tells us to adorn ourselves for the wedding feast (Mt 22:1-14). Our hope and trust must be in the timing of Christ, but we also must be prepared for either His coming or calling us home. The book of Revelation, though confusing, does have one major message that fills me with both excitement and a tinge of fear because there, Christ tells John, "I am coming soon, bringing my recompense with me, to repay each one for what he has done" (Rev 22:12).

My desire is to see Christ, but I know that when Christ returns, then the harvest is done, and the souls of the sinful will receive their punishment. That, in itself, is a sad thought because then no more can be saved. So, instead of just looking for His return, I will hope in the justice and mercy of a God who would willingly sacrifice Himself, not just for me, but for so many like me. I will pray for the salvation of those who are still lost, and I will wait on the timing of the Lord.

4

LOVE AND JUSTICE

Justice and Fairness

One of the most difficult concepts to explore is the idea of "justice" or equity. As a people, we often equate justice with fair play—even to the extent that if you look up the word in the dictionary, fair play is a synonym. But even as a child, I knew that fair play was not really justice; it could be an aspect of justice and sometimes correlate, but they were not the same thing. Fairness seems to be a feeling of "Well he got, so I should get also." But justice, especially biblical justice, doesn't appear to be synonymous with equality or governed by the feeling of "I deserve" which permeates the concept of fairness.

Mishpat, משפט, is the word most commonly translated as "just" or "justice" in the Old Testament with several other potential translations such as *judgment, law, regulations, right/righteous, standards, decisions, prescribed, requirements,* and so on. But, the most interesting thing about this word isn't what it means, but rather how it's used the first time in the entire Bible.

Instead of appearing as a word of condemnation on humanity following the fall of Adam and Eve and their expulsion from the Garden of Eden, which would make sense as they suffered the judgment of God for their sins, or as a word used against Cain after the murder of his brother Abel, or even as a word of judgment on the world for their sins prior to the flood, it appears first as a positive word much later than any of those events. The story is such a remarkable one in many ways. Abraham and Sarah were childless and too old to have children, but as they each neared the century mark on their lives, the Lord came to Abraham and Sarah and promised them a child. He did this in the form of three men appearing in front of Abraham just after the entire house was circumcised. After the visit was over, Abraham walked the men out to see them on their way, and we get a little bit of inner dialogue as the Lord discusses with Himself whether or not He will share information with Abraham:

> "Shall I hide from Abraham what I am about to do, seeing that Abraham shall surely become a great and mighty nation, and all the nations of the earth shall be blessed in him? For I have chosen him, that he may command his children and his household after him to keep the way of the Lord by doing righteousness and justice, so that the Lord may bring to Abraham what he has promised him" (Gen 18:17b-19).

Here we see God speaking about Abraham as one might about an apprentice. Abraham was chosen so that God could teach him, and then he would teach others to have both righteousness and justice. That would imply that justice, unlike fairness, is something that has clear definitions and goals rather than something that is governed by vague feelings of what constitutes equality.

I once heard Chuck Missler, a well-respected pastor, talk about why God didn't just give all of the information—the law, salvation, justification, and so on—to Adam and Eve, or even to Noah or Abraham, but waited until Moses to give the law, and used the prophets to expound on His teachings, and then even waited until Christ to truly reveal the depth and complexity of true righteousness and justice. He compared God's revelations to a parent teaching a child. Please note that this comparison has been made by many pastors and probably dates back to well before when I heard it, but this is the source of my knowledge. We don't teach a child that 2x3=6 until they understand that 3+3=6. Instead, we set the foundation which is often harder and requires more steps before we teach them the advanced method. We as a race couldn't have understood the price paid by Christ until we fully understood the sin we had committed.

God stepped us through learning right and wrong just as a parent does their child. Once we fully understood the difference, He then provided for us by His mercy a sacrifice for our sins that we may seek to be filled with righteousness and justice without fear of divine and eternal punishment for each failure. We are still called to be righteous and just. The very name we use to identify ourselves means to be "Christ-like" or like Christ; to attempt, in all areas of our lives, to live mimicking the most righteous and just man to have ever walked the earth (Mk 12:29-31; I Pet 2:21).

That being said, we know that in all fairness, we deserve what Christ received, and He deserves what we ourselves are receiving. But thankfully, we don't live in a fair world governed by a fair God, we live in a just world governed by a just God. Once the just payment had been given, we were no longer expected to pay it ourselves. Should we be living in a fair world, then it wasn't fair that Christ paid our debt. If we were governed by a fair God, then we would have to answer for what we have done without any recourse.

"How can a good God let bad things happen?"

But, how does that relate to love? Remember, as we talked about earlier, God is still a God of justice. Love doesn't negate His justice. Not to sound too much like hell-fire and damnation, but judgment is coming. The very end of the Bible gives us this warning: "I warn everyone who hears the words of the prophecy of this book … He who testifies to these things says, 'Surely, I am coming soon.' Amen. Come, Lord Jesus!" (Rev 22:18, 20). Judgment for the world is unavoidable. We know that "God will judge the righteous and the wicked" (Ecc 3:17). Because our righteousness comes from Christ (II Cor 5:21) we can ourselves rest in the very words of Abraham as he pled for any who are righteous that could have been living in the cities of Sodom and Gomorrah: "Far be it from you … to put the righteous to death with the wicked … Shall not the Judge of all the earth do what is just?" (Gen 18:25).

It's easy for those of us who know the Bible to pull up story after story of God's harsh judgments: the flood in Genesis 6-9; Sodom and Gomorrah in Genesis 18-19; the plagues in Egypt in Exodus; and the destruction of Jericho in Joshua 6. How could a loving God not only allow these things, but do them Himself? We aren't the only ones who struggle with such a question. But, as discussed in chapter 1, "God is love" (I Jn 4:8). And now, we see that God is a just God. So, how do we make these two characteristics work together?

The reason for our struggle is not because God's character seems contradictory; the reason for our struggle is because we haven't allowed ourselves to believe that love and justice are actually two sides of one coin. God's justice protects us from the wickedness of man. How could God claim to be loving if He didn't protect us from those who would harm us? At times, we all cry to the Lord with David, "Be pleased O Lord, to deliver me! O Lord, make haste to help me! Let those be put to shame and disappointed altogether who seek to snatch away my life; let those be turned back and brought to dishonor who delight in my hurt!" (Ps 40:13-14). We have all felt, either on our own behalf or on behalf of another, the pain of someone who is actively seeking to hurt us or those we love.

Perhaps, when we ask, "How can a good God let bad things happen?" we're asking the wrong question. Maybe a better question would be this: What kind of father would hear the desperate pleas of his children as they suffer at the hands of others, even unspeakable horrors, and sit back and do nothing because it would be "unloving" to the offending parties?

To put this in simpler terms, imagine a young child, maybe ten years old, running away from a bully trying to get home. He won't hit the bully because he knows it's wrong, but he doesn't want to get hit either. His one goal is to get home as quickly as he can in the hopes that his father will protect him. What kind of father would see his child running to him begging for help, and just turn his back because he "loves" the bully? God is a loving father who will intervene on our behalf. Now, to make the picture a bit clearer, imagine that the bully is also the child's brother, what then would the father do?

I know, as the fourth child of seven, some of my siblings were my worst bullies just as I bullied them, and some offenses were treated much harsher both on my behalf and on the behalf of my siblings. I remember one year, for her birthday, my older sister received a nice Barbie doll which was a rare treat (I can count on one hand how many official Barbies my sister and I got together as children). Not too long later, angry at her for some perceived or real offense (truth be told, I no longer remember what she did that made me mad), I took a pair of scissors, and with a single snip, I chopped the doll's hair off. The amount of trouble I got in was … well … appropriate to the level of the offense committed, and from that day to this, I have never doubted that I deserved what I got. But, the strange thing about the event was that my sister, who I had hurt, actually felt bad for me as I got in trouble. She didn't like it either.

Yes, sometimes that intervention seems much harsher than we would have imagined, or even wish to witness, but we also, like that 10-year-old boy, do not understand all of the ways things work yet. That punishment may be necessary for the redemption and salvation of many.

"But if our unrighteousness serves to show the righteousness of God, what shall we say? That God is unrighteous to inflict wrath on us? ... By no means! For then how could God judge the world?" (Rom 3:5-6).

Justice & Government, and God's Love

Moving forward from this idea of a father protecting his children, let's talk about one of the arms of protection He gives us: government. One of my favorite passages, though probably among the hardest for me to accept, in the New Testament comes from the epistle of Paul to the church in Rome. This is a letter that focuses on how we have been saved by the very love and mercy of God (Rom 5:8) through faith and not works. But even in such a letter, Paul has no problem communicating the hard truths we should accept.

At various times in history, we have witnessed horrible governments do horrible things to people—from the time of the ancients who sacrificed their children on idols, to the times of the Romans who squashed even the hint of a rebellion with an iron thumb and the sharp end of a sword, to the time of Stalin and Mao who massacred millions of their own people and left millions more to die from hunger for an ideal. History is filled with atrocities, but as Christians, we have been given very clear instructions:

"Let every person be subject to the governing authorities. For there is no authority except from God, and those that exist have been instituted by God. Therefore whoever resists the authorities resists what God has appointed, and those who resist will incur judgment. For rulers are not a terror to good conduct, but to bad. Would you have no fear of the one who is in authority? Then do what is good, and you will receive his approval, for he is God's servant for your good. But if you do wrong, be afraid, for he does not bear the sword in vain, for he is the servant of God, an avenger who carries out God's wrath on the wrongdoer. Therefore one must be in subjection, to only to avoid God's wrath but also for the sake of conscience" (Rom 13:1-5).

If Paul could write this in reference to the Roman government which was guilty of horrible atrocities against people (especially against those of faith), of having no sense of human rights, and in no way valuing God's Word on any matter, then maybe we need to give it a bit more weight and consider it an important passage when determining our next course of action towards our own governments.

Does that mean when given the opportunity, we should not intervene on the behalf of others? Of course not. We are in fact given an example of that. Thousands of years ago, a girl barely old enough to call grown was chosen among many because she was physically desired by the head of the kingdom. This girl, Esther, was shy and didn't share her whole life with her new husband. Instead, she kept to herself in the hopes of living as peacefully as she could. But one day, her cousin came to her and told her that, because of the jealousy of one man, her entire people were in danger. Was her life really in danger? Probably not. But all of her family and her friends were. She, like so many of us, was terrified of doing what she needed to do. But, she knew that she had been placed in a position of limited power with high influence, and with the courage given to her by God, she rose to the occasion. Her actions saved her people from the vengeful hatred of Haman (Est 8) because she took the risk and did what was right. However, it does mean that, should we find ourselves in similar positions, we should, just as in the example of Esther, do it with respect and deference because the person in authority over us was put there by God—regardless of whether that person is godly or not.

Now, don't misunderstand. The passage above is specifically addressing taxes—if you go on to read the next few verses, Paul expands on the idea. Even so, this idea of submission to governing authorities doesn't come out of the ether. Christ Himself sets up such a dialogue of submission back when the Pharisees asked about Rome's taxes: "Therefore render to Caesar the things that are Caesar's and to God the things that are God's" (Mt 22:21).

To further expand on this idea of authority and submission to authority, let's look at one of the only two times that Christ "marveled" at someone. A Centurion came to Christ to ask for His help—specifically to ask for his servant to be healed. When Christ agreed and began to go to the Centurion's home, the response was perhaps one of the most unique responses to Christ that we see in all of the gospels:

"'Lord, I am not worthy to have you come under my roof, but only say the word, and my servant will be healed. For I too am a man under authority, with soldiers under me. And I say to one, 'Go' and he goes, and to another, 'Come' and he comes, and to my servant, 'Do this' and he does it.' When Jesus heard this he marveled and said to those who followed him, 'Truly I tell you, with no one in Israel have I found such faith'" (Mt 8:8-10).

We are all ourselves under authority. Men are under the authority of the church which is made up of other men (Eph 5:21); wives are under the authority of their husbands (Eph 5:22); children are under the authority of their parents (Eph 6:1). When we learn to accept the authority over us as we have been told (Rom 13:1-5), then we ourselves can be like the Centurion who amazed Christ by his faith.

In his book on prayer, *Moving Mountains,* John Eldridge spends quite a bit of time talking about "the way things work" or working inside the system. We can't work in a system that we don't understand. First, we must place God on the throne of our hearts. Then, we must examine the structure of things around us. We must come to terms with the system which is made up of an authority structure. We are not the Alpha and Omega, Christ is (Rev 22:13). When we accept the authority of Christ, it becomes much easier for us to work within this system. When we accept the authority of the men and women around us, that also makes it easier to work within the system.

Justice and Love

Finally, let's look closer at the relationship between love and justice. We have a throne in our hearts which determines how we see the world. When God, who is love, sits on that throne, then we are able to fully understand and apply the command to love our neighbors. From the throne shoots up a tree of faith rooted firmly in God's love for us. And, sitting on top of that tree is the small, but resilient, bird that is our hope. God's justice protects all of it from outside invaders. Without His justice to guard our hearts and minds from evil, our faith in His love would wither up and die leaving the bird to find its home somewhere else.

Yes, justice is a hard reality of a world engrossed in some of the most debauched and sinful behaviors imaginable, but it is a reality we must come to terms with. And yes, sometimes the punishment seems harsher than we ourselves would dish out. But, unlike us, God can see into all men's hearts, and makes the choices that will work "for the good of those who love him, who have been called according to his purpose" (Rom 8:28 NIV). Note that it says for the good of those *who love Him*, not for the good of all mankind. Nowhere is it promised that all men will be saved, only that "all have sinned and fall short of the glory of God" (Rom 3:23) and that "many are called, but few are chosen" (Mt 22:14).

So, if God is a loving God, if He works all things together for the good of those who love Him, and if all the authority of man is given by God, then the authority placed over us is put there because God loves us, not in spite of His love. Considering that, if all authority is in fact put there also as God's arm of justice, then it follows that His justice is only another facet of His love for us. God's justice through the government is designed to be our physical protection from those that would seek to harm us.

Now, does that mean that sinful men put in places of authority won't be corrupt because they've been put there by God? As much as we all wish that was in fact the truth, it isn't. As the old adage goes: "Absolute power corrupts absolutely." Men will corrupt it, and when the outcry of God's people is heard, those governments fall. The rise and fall of many was promised by Christ Himself. The only thing that lasts forever is the fact that nothing can separate us from the sure and absolute love of God (Rom 8:38-39), and so it is that He is the only one we can put our absolute faith and trust in.

5

LOVE AND REPENTANCE

Repentance

Now that we have accepted the idea that both Love and Justice are defining characteristics of God, we have to know that we cannot, by any work of our own, be saved. We know that we are sinners and we deserve death for the sins we've committed. The fire and brimstone sermons from Jonathan Edwards are among some of the most well-known sermons in U.S. history. They, in many ways, mirrored the sermons of John the Baptist in the beginning of the New Testament, "Repent for the kingdom of heaven is at hand" (Mt 3:2). Both men, though separated by time and space, proclaimed the same message: Repent, judgment is coming.

We've all heard repentance described in many different terms—e.g., turning around, refocusing on God, turning from your sin to God, etc. Repentance is something so often called for in the Bible which requires a real consideration of what that word means and how to accomplish the goal.

A man, righteous and just and remembered as such in history, committed one of the most heinous acts recorded: he killed another man to steal his wife. David, who is described as a man after God's own heart, and ruled with the righteousness and justice of God, an ancestor of the line of Christ, arranged for the death of Uriah, one of his most trusted and supportive attendants. All of this was so he could take Uriah's wife, Bathsheba, as his own. But, even a year after the events that led to Uriah's death, David still hadn't even acknowledged what he had done. It wasn't until a theoretical issue that differed at face value was brought to him by the Lord's prophet, Nathan, that David finally confessed his sins. The actions, though evil, are not the worst things we've heard of men doing; they aren't even the worst events described in the Bible, but they are made so much worse because of the righteousness of the one who committed them. It's hard to see heroes fall.

But this fall led to perhaps one of the most beautiful Psalms of repentance available to us today. After acknowledging his sin, David turned away from it and asks God to:

"Create in me a clean heart, O God
  And renew a right spirit within me
Cast me not away from your presence
  And take not your Holy Spirit from me.
Restore to me the joy of your salvation
  And uphold me with a willing spirit."
                                    (Ps 51:10-12).

These words have been used and applied to so many different situations and people, even put into songs and referenced in poetry, so that now we often no longer even remember their origins. However, they are the basis of what the Bible says about repentance, so it's important that we understand the events leading up to the composition of this Psalm.

A king of a people at war was not with them. Instead, he was at home safe in his palace. Why he was there, no reason is given. One day, out on the roof of his home, he sees a woman bathing, and in his heart, lusts after her. That's where the sin began. After taking what he desired, she became pregnant. He tried to get her husband to sleep with her to hide the infidelity, but her husband Uriah, out of loyalty to his own men, didn't take the bait. The result was for David to use his authority to command the men Uriah was dedicated to serving to kill him by turning their backs on him. Uriah, not surprisingly, died at the betrayal of his king and his fellow soldiers, and his wife was taken by the king. The results of this were far reaching and eventually resulted in the splitting of the kingdom.

Repentance: A Biblical Definition

There is a Hebrew word בְּשׁוּבָה bə·šū·ḇāh which occurs one time in the Bible—In Isaiah—where the prophet, speaking of a rebellious people rejecting God, says, "For thus said the Lord God, the Holy One of Israel, 'In *returning* and rest you shall be saved; in quietness and in trust shall be your strength'" (15a). Using the ESV, this word is translated as *returning*, but in many other translations, it's given as *repentance*. However, regardless of what the word is translated as, it's clear that salvation depends on returning to the Lord. The use of this word is interesting because it sets up a direction.

I remember some years ago sitting in the Bible class and listening to our teacher. A straight white line of chalk went from one side of the huge blackboard to the other. In the center of that line was a single vertical line marking the midpoint. At one edge was the word "God" and the other edge "Satan." Above the line was a short, two-sided arrow labeled at each end—toward "Satan" was the word "sin" and toward "God" was the word "righteousness." I listened as he explained the theory that sin could be better described as a number line where seeking God is moving on that line in the positive directions through righteous behavior, and moving towards Satan as a negative behavior through sin. I like the analogy because it made repentance seem so much more achievable. If I couldn't be perfect, well I could still take steps towards becoming what God called me to be—someone who, like David, sought for the clean heart created only by God's grace.

I can't speak for others, but I know for myself, repentance always seemed an impossible task. I could never fully turn away from all sin, and I knew it then as much as I know it now. It seemed like when I would overcome one bad habit, I would realize that I had ten more bad habits that, often, were worse than the first. I'm a human filled with iniquity and sin; could I really turn from it? Was that even possible? But, with this new picture of sin as a direction moving away from God, then overcoming sin and repenting of my sin became a much more achievable goal. I didn't have to go from sinful to perfect, I just needed to try to move in a direction toward God. *Perfect* no longer needed to be the enemy of *good*.

This understanding revolutionized my life, and it made certain passages in the Bible so much more accessible. For instance:

> "[John] said therefore to the crowds that came out to be baptized by him, 'You brood of vipers! Who warned you to flee from the wrath to come? Bear fruits in keeping with repentance ... even now the axe is laid to the root of the trees. Every tree therefore that does not bear good fruit is cut down and thrown into the fire ... Whoever has two tunics is to share with him who has none, and whoever has food is to do likewise ... And he said to [the tax collectors] 'collect no more than you are authorized to do' ... and he said to [the soldiers] 'Do not extort money from anyone by threats or by false accusation, and be content with your wages.'" (Lk 3:7-14)

Here, John the Baptist tells these people who have been using their positions to sin to stop the sin. He doesn't tell them to stop the job, just stop using their power to hurt others. My favorite part is about the tax collectors. Jews, much like us if not more so, hated paying taxes. They thought it was unlawful and wrong. But John didn't tell the tax collectors to stop collecting taxes or to rebel against the government, he said to collect taxes in an honest fashion by only collecting the amount which were ordered to collect. So, in John's teachings, repentance meant to do what was right in the position the Lord had placed you in—be it tax collector, soldier, or layman.

But repentance can't come from our sinful hearts. We are a people of sin and iniquity, as Isaiah bemoaned that we "dwell in a people of unclean lips" (Is 6:5) and James pointed out that a man "who does not stumble in what he says ... is a perfect man, able also to bridle his whole body" (Jas 3:2). I know from personal experience, as I'm sure many others do, that control of the mouth is, in fact, impossible. Words escape us that we don't necessarily mean or fully understand all the time.

Instead, repentance must come from God. As Timothy instructed us, we should be "kind to everyone, able to teach patiently enduring evil, correcting [our] opponents with gentleness. God may perhaps grant them repentance leading to a knowledge of the truth" (II Tim 2:24-5). If repentance for our opponents comes from God, then repentance for ourselves also comes from God.

To put it another way, let's use Scripture to create a logic trail. Jesus said, "For everyone who does wicked things hates the light" (Jn 3:20), and Paul points out to the Romans, "For all have sinned and fall short of the glory of God" (3:23). If we accept those as absolute truth, then there is no way we could come to the Father except through his coming to us. Perhaps one of my favorite illustrations of this concept is in C. S. Lewis's Narnia book, *The Silver Chair*.

In the beginning of the story, Jill, a young girl at a boarding school, is being bullied by some of the other girls at school. The teachers have a "hands off" mentality that allows for this behavior. Eustace, who was introduced in the previous book *Voyage of the Dawn Treader* finds her and suggests that they escape to Narnia by calling to Aslan. Once there, they meet Aslan, but Jill doesn't know him because she hadn't seen him before. He tells them that he called for them to accomplish a specific task, but Jill becomes confused. She was certain that she and Eustace had called for Aslan, not the other way around. When she voices her question, Aslan's reply perfectly mimics how the call to repentance works: "You would not have been calling to me unless I had been calling to you" (12).

Repentance: A Picture of Christ's Love in Our Lives

—Let me insert a small disclaimer here: this is not me preaching about what should be, but rather sharing from my own personal experience the truths of God's word. I myself am a sinner like everyone else, and I claim no special righteousness because I don't have it. But I do have experience, and I think it's valuable to share that experience with others—

If we are willing to accept that sin and repentance are not so much *actions* as they are *directions* toward and away from God, and if we accept that repentance is only something we're capable of completing because of the grace of God, then what does it look like in our lives? Do either of these things mean that we don't have to worry about repentance because it's God's job? Of course not! Just like Jill and Eustace, we still have to reach for God. He's not going to do everything for us because, much as a mother teaching her child to walk, He wants us to learn on our own the benefits and rewards of reaching for Him.

Considering what we need to do and how it will look can be a bit overwhelming, but as in so many other cases, we just need to take the first step, and the rest will come as we continue moving down the road in front of us. That first step doesn't come from us, though, but rather from the Holy Spirit. The first step is a conviction of sin. This is done through the work of the Holy Spirit as promised by the prophet Jeremiah and restated by the author of Hebrews: "Behold, the days are coming ... when I will make a new covenant ... I will put my law within them and I will write it on their hearts. And I will be their God and they shall be my people" (Jer 30:31, 33b; also see Heb 8:8, 10b). In his book, *Mere Christianity*—which itself is separated into four books—C. S. Lewis spends the first book explaining that we have an innate sense of right and wrong that governs our actions; a sense of fairness that is universally understood and accepted. He also points out that we often act against that sense which we tend to refer to as our conscience, and when we do, we turn to making excuses or shifting the blame. It is my personal belief that this sense of right and wrong, at least in our early years, is the still small voice of the Holy Spirit prodding us.

At that point in our lives, we have three options. First, we could ignore it until it goes away and suffer the same kind of hardening of our hearts that Pharaoh suffered. Second, we could twist it with excuses and purposeful misinformation (in easier terms, we could lie to ourselves about what is right and wrong) until that voice is no longer capable of being heard in its original form. Or we could take the third option; we could listen to the voice and follow its guidance. That is what Jill and Eustace did in *The Silver Chair*, and what Martin Luther did as he attempted to respond to God's call, and what Samuel did when he was a small boy being called by the voice of God (I Sam 3). Our response to that voice determines which direction we move on the number line of righteousness—positive or negative.

The next part is perhaps the most difficult part of repentance and forgiveness that we must experience in this world: grief for our sins. Following the example of the Corinthians, we should be "grieved into repenting" by a "Godly grief … For Godly grief produces a repentance that leads to salvation without regret" (II Cor 7:9-10). To go back to the example of David who committed a sin with Bathsheba great enough that God took the life of their child in recompense. For seven days David "fasted and … lay … on the ground. And the elders of the house stood beside him to raise him from the ground, but he would not, nor did he eat food with them" (I Sam 12:16-17). David understood that his sin wasn't just against Uriah and Bathsheba, but also (and primarily) against the Lord (Ps 51:4). His sorrow for his sin was all consuming.

Thankfully, though, we don't have to live there long. For "If we confess our sins, he is faithful and just to forgive us our sins and to cleanse us from all unrighteousness" (I Jn 1:9). This is not just a New Testament promise though. From the beginning, God has been a loving and forgiving God. When the Israelites rebelled against God time and time again and ignored His prophets even to the point of putting them to death, even then He forgave them their transgressions:

> "But Moses said to the Lord … 'The Lord is slow to anger and abounding in steadfast love, forgiving iniquity and transgression...' Then the Lord said, 'I have pardoned, according to your word.'" (Num 14:13, 18, 20).

While both David's sin and the Israelites' sin were followed with acts of judgment, they were also promised forgiveness and redemption.

We may expect that our sins come with consequences which can be either corrective, punitive, or both. It should not be surprising that when we sin, bad things happen to us and around us. That was true even in the early church. Paul gave a warning about taking communion while living in continued sin in the church that was leading several members to sickness and even death: "That is why many of you are weak and ill, and some have died. But if we judged ourselves truly, we would not be judged" (I Cor 11:30-1). This is a warning that without repentance, there will be judgment, even for a man who has been saved by the blood of Christ.

Repentance: A Loving Celebration of Return

The final step of what repentance looks like in our lives is redemption, or restoration. It is the beautiful promise of God to restore us with a clean heart, a right spirit, and the joy of the Lord (Ps 51). If God could restore David for the sins of murder and adultery committed in the worst ways, then He can restore us too.

The parable of the Prodigal Son in Luke 15 contains some of the most beautiful imagery of restoration that we get to experience. After having stolen what wasn't yet his and squandering it, the son returns to his father's home in the hopes of at least being able to work as a servant, but the father, so pleased with the return of his son,

> "Ran and embraced him and kissed him ... the father said to his servants, 'Bring quickly the best robe, and put it on him, and put a ring on his hand, and shoes on his feet. And bring the fattened calf and kill it, and let us eat and

celebrate. For this my son was dead, and is alive
again; he was lost, and is found.' And they began
to celebrate" (Lk 15: 20b, 22-24).

There are consequences to our actions, and there
always will be. When we squander what we have, we lose
it just as the son in this story did. When we make bad
choices, bad things will happen. But, just because we go
down a bad road for a while doesn't mean that we can't
go home again.

Just as Boaz was a redeemer for Naomi and Ruth,
restoring them to the full rights and privileges of
Jewish citizenship and society, Christ is our redeemer
restoring us to the kingdom of God and the path of light
(I Cor 7:23; I Jn 1:10).

We know that "Christ redeemed us from the curse of
the law ... so that we might receive the promised Spirit
through Faith" (Gal 3:13-4). That Spirit convicts us of
sin and guides our actions if we will let it, and through
the conviction of the Holy Spirit, we are led to Christ.
Redemption comes through our reconciliation with God
through Christ: "That is, in Christ God was reconciling
the world to himself, not counting their trespasses against
them, and entrusting to us the message of reconciliation"
(II Cor 5:19). When we return to Christ by turning away
from our sins, and we begin to move in the positive direction on our number line towards God, the celebrations are
widespread and full of joy. We saw that with the prodigal
son, and we see it in other places as well:

"What man of you, having a hundred sheep, if he
has lost one of them, does not leave the ninety-
nine in the open country, and go after the one

that is lost until he finds it? And when he has found it, he lays it on his shoulders rejoicing" (Luke 15:4-5)

"Or what woman, having ten silver coins, if she loses one coin, does not light a lamp and sweep the house and seek diligently until she finds it? And when she has found it, she calls together her friends and neighbors saying, 'Rejoice with me, for I have found the coin that I had lost' " (Luke 15:8-9).

These two examples of someone seeking that which was lost precede the story of the prodigal son. They don't speak of us looking for God, but rather, they speak of God seeking us. They are among some of the most beautiful renditions of God's love for us that we see in Scripture. When He finds us, when we are returned home, then "there is joy before the angels of God over one sinner who repents" (Luke 15:10). Seek repentance under the assurance that if you ask, "it will be given to you; seek, and you will find; knock, and it will be opened to you" (Mt 7:7).

6

LOVE AND FORGIVENESS

Forgiveness

One of the most well-known passages from the ministry of Christ comes in Matthew's record when Peter asked Christ how many times a man should forgive another who has sinned against him. The response was, as my 10-year-old nephew would describe, *epic*.

> "Then Peter came up and said to him, 'Lord, how often will my brother sin against me, and I forgive him? As many as seven times?' Jesus said to him, 'I do not say to you seven times, but seventy-seven times.'" (Mt 18:22-23)

At this point, Jesus begins to tell the parable of the unforgiving servant, who, after himself being forgiven an insurmountable debt by the king, goes to a fellow servant who, by comparison, owes him almost nothing. When his fellow servant begs for at least an extension, he has the man thrown into debtor's prison. Not too long after, it's brought to the attention of the king that his servant treated his fellow servant in such a manner, so he called the insurmountable debt as due. At the end of the story, Jesus gave this warning: "So also my heavenly Father will do to every one of you, if you do not forgive your brother from your heart" (Mt 18:35).

This story demonstrates for us two major principles of Christian forgiveness. First, it demonstrates the great amount of love God has for us because He has forgiven such a massive debt that we owe Him. Second, it demonstrates for us a principle of practicing forgiveness through the love of God that we are to apply to our lives on a daily basis.

Before we get into discussing these principles, though, there is one major thing that we must first address: what is forgiveness? I, personally, have often found at times that it is easier to define a topic not by what it is, but instead by what it is not. Forgiveness is not naivete; even Christ tells us to "be wise as serpents" (Mt 10:16). Forgiveness is not about forgetting justice, but rather a release to let justice be served by God. We are never called to knowingly place ourselves or others in the path of predators because we have "forgiven" the predator for his sins against us!

In the parable of the unforgiving servant, the servant was called to release his fellow servant from debt; however, he was not told to lend money to his fellow servant again. To release someone from a debt is not the same thing as to continuously lend to one you know will default on what you give them.

Forgiveness is, instead, the internal realization and acceptance that sins which offend and hurt us are not truly against us. Sins are against God. We don't have to carry the weight of the other person's redemption. Forgiveness is a release of offended feelings and pride as well as a release of all feelings of vengeance.

Remember David's sin with Bathsheba and the murder of Uriah through Joab? Bathsheba, Uriah, and Joab were all hurt by his actions—some more than others. But, in his repentance of his sin, he doesn't beg any of them for forgiveness. Rather, he writes his Psalm to God and says, "Have mercy on me, O God … against you, you only, have I sinned and done what is evil in your sight" (Ps 51:1, 4). When we can truly release from inside ourselves that feeling of offense, and we understand that all men are guilty of sins against God, and we leave justice and vengeance to be served by God instead of by us, then we will fully be able to forgive others.

God's Forgiveness for Us

C. S. Lewis, in *Mere Christianity*, at various times talks about his life and views before he was reached by the saving grace of God. Having myself been raised a believer and accepting Christ at a relatively early age, I find some of his insights to that point in his life to be fascinating. Perhaps one of the most obvious observations he makes which I personally had never really thought about had to do with the dichotomy of the Christian view of sin. On one hand, even sins of thought—much less word or deed—are horrendous to us. We find them to be as disgusting as if we had committed the action itself: "everyone who looks at a woman with lustful intent has already committed adultery with her in his heart" (Mt 5:28).

But, on the reverse side, we talk about some of the most heinous actions as not being too much for God to forgive. We speak to murderers, adulterers, liars, and so many others proclaiming to them that, no matter what sin they've committed up to this point, Christ paid the debt for their sin. They too can find the saving grace of God. Because of my background, I have always viewed these two truths as absolute. And, rather than being contradictory, they act in concert with each other—one truth behaving as the violin and the other as the piano accompaniment. Each truth would take center-stage at a given moment, but most of the time, they complement the sounds of the other.

God's forgiveness of us, though, would always be the first seat. The power and strength would overwhelm our senses so much that until we had adjusted our ears to take in the whole melody, the rest of the song couldn't be heard. After we accept God's forgiveness, then we can move on to more beautiful things such as the maturing of what Lewis refers to as our "center self" or the maturing of our core character.

In his first epistle, the Apostle John writes to his audience a short poem where he addresses children, fathers, and young men. I find the poem itself to be a beautiful piece of writing, but I especially appreciate the message to the children: "I am writing to you, little children, because your sins are forgiven for his name's sake" (I Jn 2:12). Regardless of whether or not he is speaking to literal children or people who are still children in the faith, it doesn't matter. The first knowledge of God that we gain is that we have been forgiven of our sins.

Reaching back all the way to the dawn of time, even to the commission of the first sin, we can see God's promise of redemption and forgiveness. The first Messianic prophecy happens before the punishment of the sin is given when God tells the serpent, "I will put enmity between you and the woman, and between your offspring and her offspring; he shall bruise your head, and you shall bruise his heel" (Gen 3:15). Imagine it in more modern terms. A small child wants to play on his parent's phone, so he goes and takes it off the charger knowing that he's not supposed to do that because he should be working on his schoolwork. When it comes out that the phone was removed from the charger and used for games when it wasn't supposed to be, obviously there are consequences. Perhaps the parent grounds the child from the phone for a few days. The implicit promise is that this is a temporary measure that will be lifted in a short time. This verse of punishment for the serpent was the same for Adam and Eve—a promise that the consequences would be short-lived, that there is an end to the pain and suffering caused by their choice, that there will be forgiveness and redemption in the future.

That is the long-term promise of forgiveness for all people, but there are more immediate promises of forgiveness from God that we have been given such as:

"If we confess our sins, he is faithful and just to forgive us our sins and to cleanse us from all unrighteousness" (I Jn 1:9)

"In him we have redemption through his blood, the forgiveness of our trespasses, according to the riches of his grace which he lavished upon us in all wisdom and insight" (Eph 1:7-8).

"Bless the Lord, O my soul, and forget not all his benefits, who forgives all your iniquity" (Ps 103:2-3a).

"And the Holy Spirit also bears witness to us; for after saying, 'This is the covenant that I will make with them after those days, declares the Lord: I will put my laws on their hearts, and write them on their minds,' then he adds, 'I will remember their sins and their lawless deeds no more.' Where there is forgiveness of these, there is no longer any offering for sin" (Heb 10:15-8).

With even the Holy Spirit as our witness, we have been promised the forgiveness of God by His grace and love.

Our Forgiveness of Others

Forgiveness, however, is one of the more unique promises made to us. Unlike the promises of grace and love, forgiveness comes with a stipulation. Even in the Lord's Prayer, He tells us to pray, "and forgive us our debts, as we also have forgiven our debtors" (Mt 6:12). Right after sharing the model on how we should pray, Christ warns those listening to Him that "if you do not forgive others their trespasses, neither will your Father forgive your trespasses" (Mt 6:15). The not-so-subtle implication, much like love, then is that forgiveness is not a feeling, but rather an action that we ourselves can, in fact, control. So, how do we forgive others?

Earlier, I mentioned a moment of realization that I had where I realized that the weight of bitterness I had been carrying due to my lack of forgiveness had been removed from me, but I want to go a bit more in detail in the hopes that this will help someone who reads the story. Without going too much into the many darker aspects of my life, I do want to share with you my story of healing because it came from Christ, and nothing else could have freed me from that weight.

At the beginning of this book, I hinted at some of the abuse that I experienced when I was a child. Following the death of my father just before my fifth birthday, my family moved across the country where my mother met and married my step-father. He had successfully convinced her that he was a believer when, in fact, he wasn't. Instead, he was a man who liked having weak people under him and he was physically abusive to me and my brother—though not to the older children as they were able to stand up for themselves. At the same time, I was also being sexually molested by another man who had my mother's trust. Both forms of abuse lasted years, and the damage caused by them still follows me today. I write this not to condemn these two men, but so that the rest of what I say has a context.

My journey of learning about both bitterness and forgiveness finds its root here. Bitterness colored me and my interactions with others for so long that I no longer even noticed that it was there. It was also during this time that I came to Christ. While I could use age and lack of understanding as an excuse for my inability to forgive, once I was old enough to hold a grudge, I was old enough to forgive, but I chose to hold a grudge. I would probably date the formation of my root of bitterness to around the age of 13, some five years following the events, because it was at that time the memories which had been suppressed began to reappear.

Every offense against me, whether perceived or real, that happened following the re-emergence of my traumas began to pile on top of those memories. For years, I let the feelings of bitterness grow unchecked and unlimited until one day, when I was about 19 years old, I found myself sitting in church legitimately wondering, "How do we forgive? How do we let these offenses go?" As I contemplated this question, I found many pieces of advice flowing my way … *forgive because God forgave you… every time you think of the offense, forgive it; even if you're forgiving them every day … forgive yourself … realize that your offender was a child …* etc. None of that worked, and in many cases, felt a little bit like I was just running in circles around the issue. It was as if the question "How do we forgive?" was being answered with "We forgive by forgiving." If you have ever felt this way, please know you're not the only one. I was in the same place for more years than I care to count.

But, what do we do from that lost position of circular reasoning?

I can't say what works for everyone, but I can talk about what worked for me. In my position, I was unable to "forgive" just by forgiving as I felt I was being told to do. Instead I found myself praying, almost with the same desperation of a beggar, for God to show me how to forgive because I was so exhausted from the weight I had to carry. For an offense as great as the ones I was trying to forgive, it's also wise to ask for help—to ask others to listen, to pray, and to be there for you. We are not individuals in the church who have to "pick ourselves up by our bootstraps." We are the body of Christ, and we don't have to face these things alone. Rather than telling yourself that you're not a Christian because you are struggling to forgive an offense, ask God to give you the strength and direction to forgive and ask others in the body of Christ to pray with and for you as well. We are called the *body* of Christ because we are one organism meant to work together and to help each other.

My best description of what worked for me is this: I viewed those two men through the lens of the cross of Christ. I considered their fallen nature through the lens of God's love. It came some months after I truly began to work on putting God on the throne of my heart. Forgiveness was no longer the action I was trying to achieve, but rather, the love of God was what I was trying to share. And once God was the center of my world, forgiveness just followed.

Even to this day, I'm certain that forgiveness came only because Christ gave me the strength to forgive. The story of the day that Corrie ten Boom stood face to face with one of her jailers and how she describes it being only by the strength of God that she was able forgive is a perfect example of what I felt. It was truly only the strength of God that allowed me to move past this and experience the relief of true forgiveness.

When I was finally able to truly, from the heart, forgive him for the offense, I found it had no effect on how I viewed him. He is today, to me, the same as he was all those years ago when I held the grudge mostly against him. I could never trust him, and I see no support for such a position in God's word. My perspective didn't change; I didn't readjust my point of view. Instead, when forgiveness came to me, I found that it was more of a movement of responsibility. I was no longer responsible to make sure that justice would be done. I was no longer responsible for the actions done against me. I was no longer the one that my offender had to answer to. Instead, all of that falls to God, and I get the benefit of absolute trust that true justice will be served on my behalf. That sin, itself, will be thrown into the lake of fire. When I was finally able to let go, I found myself caught in the hands of God, and that's where I've been ever since.

But, the relief was even greater than I could imagine. All of those perceived and real offenses that had been piling up for years—the records I had kept of every time someone had done me wrong and I had tried so many times to forget in the past—they were all gone. Once the root was cut off, all of the leaves died out.

In the Lord's Prayer in Matthew 6, we ask for many things—God's will to be done, our daily bread, forgiveness, guarding us against temptation, deliverance from evil—but only one request depends on our own behavior: Forgiveness. The reason for this isn't so much because God is spiteful or petty thinking things such as "well if you're going to do that to your brother, then I'll show you!" Instead, I believe the requirement of request (that we forgive before we're forgiven) is more about God's love for us. We have already determined that God is love (I Jn 4:9) and that love isn't an action or feeling, but rather the lens through which we see the world. If God sees us through His love for us, then He could only want what's best for us. Ridding ourselves of bitterness, hate, anger, and envy (all of the things caused by a lack of forgiveness) makes us happier.

Just as a mother makes a child unhappy in a moment by limiting their junk food because she knows that a child who eats healthy will, in the long run, be happier, so God also knows that we will be better for having forgiven our fellow man—be he Christian or not—so He withholds His gift until we've done what is best for us.

Giving vs. Asking for Forgiveness

As Christians, there is an extra step we have to consider. We, as Christians, are called to repent of sin and to ask for forgiveness, not only from God, but also from all who we have offended:

> "So if you are offering your gift at the altar and there remember that your brother has something against you leave your gift there before the altar and go. First be reconciled to your brother, and then come and offer your gift" (Mt 5:23-4).

By the very instructions of Christ, we are called to seek reconciliation and forgiveness from others. From early childhood, we learn that when we do something bad such as hit a sibling, Mom makes us go back to our sibling and apologize. Often, after the apology, our sibling has to say "I forgive you." While this may be a great way to teach young children the process of repentance and forgiveness, it is not always so useful to adults.

We, as adults, cannot hold our forgiveness back until we have been apologized to. In my own personal example, in the nearly thirty years that have passed since the offense, I have not yet been apologized to. That used to make me angry because the person has had several chances to apologize, but they haven't. If I withheld my forgiveness until I received an apology, I might withhold it until the second coming of Christ. It does no good to wait for an apology. Forgiveness has to be given regardless of the other person's willingness to ask for it.

Now, when dealing with Christians, we are in fact given a protocol of behavior. In Matthew 18:15-20, we are provided with very specific directions on how to deal with severe offenses committed by Christians. First, we go to the offender privately. If that doesn't change anything, we take another person or two with us and go to them again. If the sin continues, we take the church leadership with us. Should it continue even then, we are called to separate ourselves from the offender. Does that mean to stop showing love to the offender (praying for their repentance and salvation) or to not forgive the offender? No! It just means to protect ourselves and those around us, we are to separate from them until fruit of repentance has been seen.

Forgiveness is truly one of the most freeing experiences while one of the hardest commands to follow. It requires absolute trust in God as well as the ability to look at those who hate us, despise us, hurt us, and so much more, through eyes that see God's love and desire for that person to be saved. Forgiveness can't come from our own strength, but from God for we know that we "can do all things through him who strengthens" us (Phil 4:13).

7

LOVE, SACRIFICE, AND HUMILITY

Possessions and the Bible

Have you ever noticed that some of the richest people, that is, the people who seem to have everything, are some of the unhappiest people? I know that I have. And some of the happiest people I've ever met seem to have nothing. The songs attribute this to "love," and I think they're more correct than they realize. The truly happy people that I have had the privilege of meeting have had one thing in common: they love enough to sacrifice everything they have for God.

One of the reasons these people are able to just enjoy the life around them without fear of losing what they have is that they view themselves more as God's stewards, as ones who have been given a particular task of caretaker for the things in their lives. They treat them as the men in the parable of the talents in Matthew 25 trying to be as the man who had five talents so that when the day comes, they may hear Christ say, "Well done, good and faithful servant. You have been faithful over a little, I will set you over much. Enter into the joy of your master" (Mt 25:21).

Rather than attaching ourselves to fear of losing what we have, we should always remember to view what we have as God's possessions. We only have what we have because it was given to us by God. As John told his disciples, "A person cannot receive even one thing unless it is given him from heaven" (Jn 3:27). Everything we have comes from God and is a gift for us to enjoy. As the wisest man in history wrote:

> "Go, eat your bread with joy, and drink your wine with a merry heart, for God has already approved what you do. Let your garments be always white. Let not oil be lacking on your head. Enjoy life with the wife whom you love, all the days of your vain life that he has given you under the sun, because that is your portion in life and in your toil at which you toil under the sun. Whatever your hand finds to do, do it with your might, for there is no work or thought or knowledge or wisdom in Sheol, to which you are going." (Ecc 9:7-10).

That being said, we know we have been blessed with the gifts in our life for our enjoyment, and as such, we should enjoy them. Not long before my father passed away in a car accident, he gave my sister a white stuffed fluffy dog (he gave me and my brother things as well, but we were too young for the impact to last). Now, thirty years later, my sister still has that dog; she treasures it and enjoys it.

That is how our things are to be treated, as treasured gifts from someone who loves us and wants us to be happy.

Now, I have seen from personal experience that treasuring the gifts we've received from God can go too far. Some people, believing themselves stewards of things that belong to God, can become so overprotective of their things on God's behalf that they behave worse than those who are just greedy. They view each damage to their things as a personal affront against God, and often, those things that they are *guarding* for God become hidden away much as the servant with the single talent. Sure, they can in fact hand back to God that which was His, but the response from Christ is harsh: "You wicked and slothful servant! You knew...! Then you ought to have invested my money with the bankers, and at my coming should have received what was my own with interest ... cast the worthless servant into the outer darkness. In that place there will be weeping and gnashing of teeth" (Mt 25:26, 30).

The right answer, like so many answers in the Bible, is to come at it with a view of humility. We are to accept and enjoy the gifts God has given us, but we are also to view ourselves as stewards and not possessors. If we do it successfully, we can "show [ourselves] in all respects to be a model of good works" (Titus 2:7).

Open-Handed Acceptance

Once we have truly internalized and accepted that everything we have is God's, and once we view ourselves as stewards rather than possessors, we can reap the benefits of contentment. We learn to ask for things and to hold onto that which we already have with open hands;

turning their well-being and security over to God rather than trying with all our might to grasp them and hold. Many great men had to learn this lesson the hard way, but once they accepted that God was in control, God was able to reward them with so much they didn't know what to do.

Abraham was tested to an extent beyond even what we could imagine. God told him to "Take your son, your only son, Isaac, whom you love, and go to the land of Moriah, and offer him there as a burnt offering on one of the mountains of which I shall tell you" (Gen 22:2). Understanding that Abraham had waited literally a century for the blessing of a child, and Isaac was the promised child that came through Sarah, we know that such a request, especially from the God who had promised that he would in fact be the father of a great many nations through this son, had to have been devastating. The days it took to travel to the location, knowing what he was going to have to do, must have been some of the darkest days of his life. But Abraham assumed, and rightly so, that God would still keep His promise and, with open hands, gave his son back to God (Heb 11:17-19).

Another person tested who, with a closed tight fist, held onto what he was given for fear of losing it, and who God had to push until his hand was loosened was Jacob. After having lost Rachel's first son, Joseph, to what Jacob, at the time, believed was death at the sharp claws of wild animals, he held Benjamin, Rachel's remaining son, even closer to himself with a tight fist of protection. When the ruler of Egypt (who was Joseph in disguise) kept one of the brothers to ensure that the other brothers would return with Benjamin, even then Jacob refused to release his hold on the youngest son. Eventually, when he was at risk of losing them all, he said "Take also your brother and arise, go again to the man. May God Almighty grant you mercy before the man and may he send back your other brother and Benjamin" (Gen 43:13-4). Once Jacob released his hold on Benjamin, he was rewarded not only with the return of Benjamin, but also Simeon who had been held in Egypt during the interim, and Joseph, the one whom Jacob had thought to be dead.

Job also was a great man in the eyes of God. But even so, he lost a great amount of his possessions, friends, and family. He lost almost all of his children, almost every possession he owned, his wife turned from him, and his friends condemned him. For a long while, he begged God to tell him what was going on, and at one point, became almost accusatory to God. But, once he released everything into the keeping of God, God restored to him double what he had lost during the trial.

A few chapters earlier, I referenced C. S. Lewis's book *The Great Divorce* specifically referencing a discussion that took place between a brother and sister. They were talking about her dead son, Michael. It's perhaps one of the best explanations for this release of our own wants, desires, and loves that we can read. Pam, the spirit from the lower world (hell), and her brother, Reginald, who appears as a "bright spirit" from heaven are talking about Pam's son, Michael. Reginald is trying to tell his sister how she might be able to see Michael again, and he says:

"I'm afraid the first step is a hard one," said the Spirit. "But after that you'll go on like a house on fire. You will become solid enough for Michael to perceive you when you learn to want someone else besides Michael. I don't say 'more than Michael,' not as a beginning. That will come later. It's only the little germ of a desire for God that we need to start the process" (Lewis 90)

When we are able to fully release our desires into God's keeping, we can say with Paul, "I know how to be brought low, and I know how to abound. In any and every circumstance, I have learned the secret of facing plenty and hunger, abundance and need" (Phil 4:12). The secret is to sacrifice all we have to God, and then He is free to bless us.

Pride and Arguments

In the third section of his book *Mere Christianity*, Lewis has a chapter titled "The Great Sin" which he uses to talk about the sin of Pride. Many of our sins in life can be traced back to this particular feeling. Even phrases such as "That's beneath me," or "I won't deign that with an answer" (even the phrases that we tell our children to motivate them to walk away from conflict) find their root in pride.

Don't get me wrong, we absolutely shouldn't engage in frivolous arguments and useless conflicts. Instead, we should take to heart the advice Paul gives to Timothy when he says, "Have nothing to do with foolish, ignorant controversies; you know that they breed quarrels. And the Lord's servant must not be quarrelsome, but kind to everyone, able to teach, patiently enduring evil" (II Tim 2:23-4).

Instead of proving that we're right in these arguments, we should seek to humbly represent God in the best way possible. Sometimes, some things aren't worth addressing, and other times, we need to take a stand. How do we determine those? The best answer I can give you is to seek God. When heresy begins to enter the church, we should definitely take a stand, but when we disagree with someone over economic choices made by the government, it might be a time to back off and say, "I disagree with you, but I still love you because we are all God's people." There are other times when it is pointless to argue or debate with someone.

In reading *Sitting at the Feet of Rabbi Jesus*, I had a particular Scripture opened up to me in a way I had never heard before. Jewish teachers of Jesus' time would use keywords to connect various Scriptures. For instance, the Hebrew word for Noah's Ark is the same word used to describe the basket that baby Moses was put into so he could be hidden from the Egyptians. Those two places are the only places in the first five books of the law that word appears, so when using that word, Jews would immediately think of both of those very well-known stories. Using the same word to introduce another teaching would automatically connect those two stories with the point being made. This was called "stringing pearls."

With that understanding, consider Jesus' words when He said, "Do not give dogs what is holy, and do not throw your pearls before pigs, lest they trample them underfoot and turn to attack you" (Mt 7:6). Arguing a point trying to prove ourselves right to someone who refuses to consider or listen is pointless, and instead, it will make us a target. This can be seen even in the current world today where people are being shunned and threatened for political and religious beliefs. Our pride is not worth the argument, and we should only seek to serve God.

If our goal is God, and He is the one sitting on the throne of hearts, the arguments that matter will be taken care of by God. Christ promises that when it's important, He "will give [us] a mouth and wisdom which none of [our] adversaries will be able to withstand or contradict" (Luke 21:15). We don't have to worry about what we'll say in these situations, we only need to seek God and let everything else be worked out by Him.

But, we as humans, often want to be right, to have the last word. We don't want to turn things over to God because that means that the other person might, for a minute, conclude that we think they're right! How could we let that happen? Wouldn't such a thing be an affront to God, even blasphemous? Well yes, it would be if our god is pride. If our self-righteousness and our pride sit on the throne of our hearts, then yes, to sit back and not argue would be an impossible task. But that's not what we who proclaim Christ are called to be.

Of course, we don't spend our lives groveling before everyone while proclaiming our own worthlessness. That kind of behavior is also a display of pride because, much like the Pharisees' behavior in the parable Christ told about the Pharisee and the tax collector, it serves to do nothing more than to draw more attention to ourselves.

But, much like forgiveness, the answer to ridding ourselves of pride is to not be prideful. How do we do that? I like C. S. Lewis's response to this when he addresses what he calls "The Great Sin" of Pride: "In God you come up against something which is in every respect immeasurably superior to yourself. Unless you know God as that—and, therefore, know yourself as nothing in comparison—you do not know God at all" (Lewis 111). The answer of how to overcome pride is to see God as who He really is, and then we will have no room left to be full of pride.

Love and Humility

Moving instead to the antithesis of pride, we find ourselves looking at humility. The very act of ridding ourselves of pride turns us into humble people. We are no longer filled with the desire to be the center of attention or the most important person in the room. Instead, we step back and allow other people to take the space. Obviously, there are times when we are still called to stand up for righteousness and for the weak. We're not called to be timid little church mice, we're called to be soldiers for God.

At the same time, we're called to "do nothing from selfish ambition or conceit, but in humility count others more significant than [our]selves. Let each of [us] look not only to his own interests, but also to the interests of others" (Phil 2:3-4). True humility is invisible to the onlooker, but visible to God. It removes the leaven of pride from us, and allows others to have the right of way, to be right, to be heard, and instead, focuses itself on seeking God and giving glory to God for all things. When we stand up for ourselves, it shouldn't be for our own sakes, but for the sake of Christ and for His kingdom.

I have heard it said by many that if you think you're humble, then you're not. But, at that point, I come to the same place of confusion that I did with both love and forgiveness. If it's true that to think I'm humble is a sign that I'm not, then how do I attempt to follow the command to walk humbly with my God (Mic 6:8)? How can I know that the choices I'm making are done with humility? The answer to that is a lot simpler than people realize. If we want to examine ourselves to determine if we are acting humbly, we only need to ask if we're acting in love.

Humility is the character trait that allows us to love, and so comes before love. Just as we mentioned earlier, it is coming up against God, the supreme and all-powerful being that created everything that we know from nothing, and the realization that we're nothing in comparison to such greatness that allows us to consider that we're not the most important person to have ever existed. As a result, love cannot be the outworking of our lives until we have humility in our hearts.

In many ways, love and humility cover the same ground. True love, the kind of love that comes from having Christ seated on the throne in our hearts, leads to humility because "Love is patient and kind; love does not envy or boast; it is not arrogant or rude. It does not insist on its own way; it is not irritable or resentful; it does not rejoice at wrongdoing, but rejoices with the truth" (I Cor 13:4-6). Isn't that also the definition of true humility?

To expand a bit more, humility is the character trait that allows us to sacrifice all that we have for the glory of God. It was Abraham's humility, his complete understanding that God is so much more powerful and able to do that which Abraham cannot even comprehend, that gave him the courage and trust, and to be willing to sacrifice Isaac. It was Jacob's begrudging humility at the realization that he could not, on his own, save his family from the famine by which he was able to have Joseph restored to him. It was Job's humility at the end of his suffering that allowed him to turn his trust over to God and to be restored.

Pride is the thing that moves our mouths before we can stop it, that prevents us from trust or from experiencing God's love for ourselves. It is humility that allows us to see the world for what it truly is. And so, I find my hope being that I will one day be able to fully embrace the same pride that Paul had so that I can say with him: "For I will not venture to speak of anything except what Christ has accomplished through me" (Rom 15:18); or, in simpler terms, let us only be proud of the work Christ does through us for others.

8

LOVE, JOY, AND PEACE

Anxiety and Love

Before I can begin this chapter which deals with peace and joy, I have to address the very antithesis of these two concepts: anxiety. To be honest, this is a hard section for me to write because it is one of my personal weaknesses. This particular behavior runs in my family and is often the topic of "coffee" talk that I have with my mother and sister when we get together in the mornings. Being that this book is written in the summer of 2020, I'm sure many people reading this know what may be causing excessive anxiety for several of us. Just to put this in perspective, at my worst, my anxiety was causing me to miss work, and sometimes to even leave work in the middle of the day (anyone who's been a teacher knows what that means … it's no small thing to get a substitute teacher for the second half of the day that is already half over). Without going too much into the anxiety triggers,

I want to talk a bit about some of the things I have learned, and what works as well as what doesn't.

The first thing I want to address are some of the "techniques" that I have been given that don't truly work. The main one is *ignore it, it will go away ... no one can live in a state of anxiety, so it must go away.* This is a horrible piece of advice and obviously given from someone who either hasn't experienced real anxiety or has a greater capacity to compartmentalize than I have ever been blessed with. Another one is *it's not that bad, just let it go!* This also didn't work for me. I knew it wasn't worth the emotional strain when I was feeling it, and being told what I already knew wasn't helpful. While these pieces of advice were given with good intent, they often exacerbated my issues rather than fixing them.

A half-way helpful piece of advice was *just change your perspective ... look at God and you'll be okay.* This was half-way helpful because it was what set my feet moving in a useful direction, but it didn't actually tell me how to do it. I'm a very practical and realistic minded person, and so I need very real and concrete directions, not just big ideas or concepts. I knew this idea was right; I knew that if I could shift my perspective to focus on God, then I would in fact successfully overcome my fear and anxiety. But how do we do that? The technique that worked for me was to follow the command to rejoice and the directions for how to obtain peace as I've outlined them below.

Joy and Gratitude

One of my favorite movies when I was a child was the Disney movie *Pollyanna*. In it, a young girl who is orphaned by her missionary parents, travels to a small town to live with her very wealthy aunt. While it has been many years since I saw the movie, one scene still floats very clearly in my mind's eye:

In this scene, we find the pastor of the church in this community out in the fields preparing his sermon for the week. Pollyanna's aunt has sent her to deliver a note to the pastor who, though he hadn't noticed it, had allowed the church to fall into the sin of preferentialism that James gives a strong warning against in his epistle. The note contained "suggested" verses for Sunday's sermon—which really meant that these were the verses Pollyanna's aunt wanted to hear read from the pulpit on the coming Sunday—but before he reads the note, he and Pollyanna talk for a few minutes. In the conversation, Pollyanna, in her innocent way, tells him that she thinks he should talk more about joy and thanksgiving because the Bible talks about joy and thanksgiving; as a matter of fact, she says her father found well over 800 times that the Bible tells us to be happy and rejoice.

Between the timing of her conversation with him and his own growing character, we see a phenomenal change take place that she doesn't even notice as she skips back to other activities. Hours later, his wife finds him in the fields with his forehead sporting a bright red sunburn because he had been out there the whole time praying for forgiveness and redemption. The movie itself focuses a great amount of time on spreading joy and being happy because that's what God wants for us, and this scene drives home the message for me. Despite its subtleness, this scene was the climactic moment of the movie, and from that point forward, there is a great change in the direction of the movie.

In writing this book, though, my own curiosity got to me. While I have not gone through and counted the times myself, I did want to have at least an idea of the scope of the command to be joyful. So, I chose one word that would communicate that: Rejoice. I chose this word because it is an imperative rather than just talking about someone experiencing joy. The word *rejoice* (including *rejoiced, rejoices,* and *rejoicing*) appears nearly 200 times in the NIV Bible. This count doesn't include words such as joy, happiness, glad, or any other rendition of the same idea. Well over half of the occurrences of this word are commands to "Rejoice in God" or "Rejoice with Israel" or "Rejoice, O Gentiles." We are told to rejoice in the good times out of gratitude because we have been blessed, and we are to rejoice in suffering because we are blessed to share in the sufferings of the saints. Over and over we are told to rejoice in the Lord.

That kind of joy is only possible once we have rid ourselves of the sin of pride and the weight of bitterness. Once we're free of those, we have the room to experience real and true joy as given to us by Christ. The true joy that is the gift of God goes much deeper than a surface-level happiness. Those days when we are feeling light and happy and everything seems to be right with the world are great, but we are called to be joyful on the darkest days. Paul gives us directions on how to do that in his letter to the Philippians:

> "Rejoice in the Lord always; again I will say rejoice. Let your reasonableness be known to everyone. The Lord is at hand; do not be anxious about anything, *but in everything by prayer and supplication with thanksgiving let your requests be*

made known to God. And the peace of God, which surpasses all understanding will guard your hearts and your minds in Christ Jesus" (Phil 4:4-7 emphasis added).

Joy comes from seeking God and turning all of our anxiety and worries over to Him through prayer. Prayer is complete only if it includes thanksgiving for the things that we do have. As silly as the joyful game Pollyanna played was, it is truly effective because it teaches us to look at what we have rather than wishing for what we don't have.

As someone who has suffered with great anxiety and fear over my life—as I mentioned at the beginning of this chapter—I can personally attest to how difficult of a task that can be. But I don't want to focus this chapter on anxiety so much as joy, which is the key to overcoming anxiety. Don't think that I'm attempting to say that to experience joy we must not be anxious, and to not be anxious we must experience joy. While joy releases us from fear, the key to finding joy is gratitude. Not the simple "thank you" gratitude that we give when someone passes us the sugar bowl, but the real, heartfelt, deep gratitude that we experience in response to some of the most loving acts we have received.

When we approach God, it is not in fear and trembling—as we are called to work out our salvation—but instead, we are called to "enter his gates with thanksgiving and his courts with praise! Give thanks to him; bless his name!" (Ps 100:4). When we come to God, our first and foremost priority is to praise Him. Thankfulness allows us to remind ourselves of the good He has done for us. As we know from personal experience, it is so easy to forget when someone does something nice for you, but it's very easy to remember all of the wrong. Christians are no different in their memory of God, so it is beneficial for us to spend time remembering all of our blessings.

By putting God first and focusing on His blessings, we have the benefit of reminding ourselves of events, items, and people that make us happy. One of the sweetest pleasures I have as an aunt to children who are being raised to know Christ is to listen to their prayers. It's so cute to hear an 8-year-old tell God how thankful he is for his family and friends, and then to have them spend a good ten minutes listing every name of the people he's thankful for. Sometimes, in our hubbub of maturity, we lose sight of all that we really have. Instead we should be like the children around us, and learn to apply gratitude. The actual practice of gratitude is as old as time; and a biblical gratitude dates back to the beginning of God's people. We are loved; we should never forget to be thankful for the love we experience.

The history of God's people has been one act of love on God's part after another. He has rescued them and forgiven them and provided redemption for them over and over again. And through His people, God brought about the redemption of the world. Through His chosen people, Christ Himself came to Earth and sacrificed everything in an act of love that far exceeds anything we ourselves could ever mimic. If we agree with the testimony of Paul and accept that Christ did in fact die for our sins (I Cor 15:3-8), then we know that there is a gift far greater than anything else that we can be thankful for even if we should lose everything around us.

A practice I learned from the book *Sitting at the Feet of Rabbi Jesus* that helps me to remember to be thankful—at least, when I'm consistent about it—is to offer short specific prayers of thanksgiving to God throughout the day for everything that happens. If I walk outside and the sun is shining, then I thank Him for the sunshine; if it's raining, then I thank Him for the rain. This is a practice the Jews had long before Christ, and some of the more observant Jews still carry on today. It's a practice called *brakha* which means *blessing*, and it comes from a reminder that Moses gave the Israelites to "bless the Lord your God for the good land he has given you" (Deut 8:10). Spangler and Tverberg expand on the idea in their book by talking about "Saturating Your Life in Prayer." The practice has had a profound effect on my life because it set up a habit of always taking everything to God. Being thankful for what He gives me reminds me that there is always something to rejoice about even when times are hard.

Peace and Joy

Joy and peace are some of the greatest experiences we have in this life. No matter what's going on outside of us, we can always experience these because they happen regardless of our situations.

Hours before writing this, I attended a funeral for my great uncle (my maternal grandfather's brother-in-law). His wife, JoAnn, is the last survivor of my grandfather's 11 siblings. In my life, I have attended numerous funerals ranging in relation from my own father's as a child, to friends', to distant and close relations, and others. I have gone to funerals of people that I know and people that I don't know. Some of these people have been saved, and some have not.

It has been many years for me since the last time I went to the funeral of a person who was saved, of a person who I know I will see again, and I found that it was different than those I had recently attended. I have matured personally and released much of my own bitterness and anger, and that has had a profound effect on how I view the world and those around me. It's not that anything happened to make my understanding of the truth different, but rather that I was now free from the baggage I had chosen to carry, and now I could see it in truth. While my uncle was a good man, I haven't been close to him in my life, so there is some distance from the personal connection. However, I do love him as both a family member and a brother in Christ. But, for perhaps the first time in my life, I was able to view a person's passing with peace because I was no longer focused on myself. My pain ... my bitterness ... they were no longer important. With the release of my bitterness, I was able to truly feel the "peace of God which surpasses all understanding" (Phil 4:7).

Inner peace, unlike forgiveness or even joy, is not a command given to us; it is a blessing that we receive. Epistle after epistle starts and even ends with the blessing of peace (Rom 1:7; 16:20; I Cor 1:3; I Cor 16:21; II Cor 1:2; 13:11-12; Gal 1:3; Eph 1:2; 6:23-4; Phil 1:2; Col 1:2; I Th 1:1; 5:23; II Th 1:2; 3:16; I Tim 1:2; II Tim 1:2; Tit 1:4; Phil 1:3; Heb 13:20; I Pet 1:2; 5:14; II Pet 1:2; II John 1:3; Jude 1:2). Now, I know this seems pointless because these are all just greetings and a few strokes of a pen to follow "polite" society. But to dismiss any words in the Bible as empty or hollow is a dangerous path to follow, because then you're left to wonder what was "polite" and what was real. The only way the Bible has any credence is if it is the true, complete Word of God. If we accept that as fact, then no words in the Bible are hollow for "polite" society. Note that several epistles are left off the list, and not all of them have it at the beginning, and many of them do not end with a blessing of peace. But, they are there several times, and they are not commands. They read as blessings bestowed on the church such as "Grace to you and peace from God our Father and the Lord Jesus Christ" (II Th 1:2).

A blessing in the old testament was not a wish or a desire or 'bestowing good favor' as it seems to be today. A blessing in the old testament was treated almost as an inheritance. It was given from father to son (and sometimes from grandfather to grandson) and from the priests to the people. Some well-known examples include Abraham and Melchizedek (priestly blessing):

"And Melchizedek king of Salem brought out bread and wine. (He was a priest of God Most High). And he blessed him and said, 'Blessed be Abram by God Most High, Possessor of heaven and earth; and blessed be God Most High, who has delivered your enemies into your hand!' " (Gen 14:18-20)

Isaac and Jacob (parental blessing):

" 'See the smell of my son is the smell of a field that the Lord has blessed! May God give you of the dew of heaven and of the fatness of the earth and plenty of grain and wine. Let peoples serve you, and nations bow down to you. Be lord over your brothers, and may your mother's sons bow down to you. Cursed be everyone who curses you, and blessed be everyone who blesses you!'" (Gen 27:27-9)

Jacob to Manasseh and Ephraim (blessing from a grandparent):

"So he blessed them that day, saying, 'By you Israel will pronounce blessings, saying, 'God make you as Ephraim and as Manasseh.'"

These are blessings in the sense meant by biblical writers. Having these in mind, read Paul's words and see if they have a similar tone to them: "Now may the Lord of peace himself give you peace at all times in every way" (II Th 3:16). When we are given blessings by God, they are given freely and by God's grace. It's without reason but, I would warn, not without requirement.

If there's one thing that my life has taught me, there are *no* requirements for God's love, but there *may be* requirements for God's blessings. Various promises of God are in fact given with stipulations—or more precisely, instructions—on how to obtain them, and peace is no different. Look closer at this passage that I quoted in the earlier part of this chapter:

"Rejoice in the Lord always; again I will say rejoice. Let your reasonableness be known to everyone. The Lord is at hand; do not be anxious about anything, but in everything by prayer and supplication with thanksgiving let your requests be made known to God. And the peace of God, which surpasses all understanding will guard

your hearts and your minds in Christ Jesus"
(Phil 4:4-7).

Let's consider this in a different mindset. Instead of
separate items that are unrelated to each other, let's think
about it as a set of directions to experience God's peace.
If that's the case, it might read more like the following:

(1) Always rejoice in the Lord.
(2) Be reasonable with and to everyone.
(3) Don't be anxious about anything—the Lord is
    here with you.
(4) Turn everything over to the Lord with prayer.
(5) Give thanks even in your prayers.

Now, if you do all of those steps, then, and only
then, will you be blessed with "the peace of God, which
surpasses all understanding." God doesn't promise
unconditionally to give us peace no matter what we do,
think, or say. Because God uses guilt, shame, and other
unpleasant, peace-reducing emotions to help correct
us, such a promise would be the equivalent of telling a
3-year-old that you will never be in trouble! Not a wise
choice; but thankfully, we serve a wise God.

However, as a wise and loving God, He does give us
directions on how to obtain peace just as loving parents
tell their children what to do *before* they get in trouble
rather than after. We have only to follow the directions
we've been given, and we will experience the full blessing
of God just as James told us: "But the one who looks into
the perfect law, the law of liberty, and perseveres, being
no hearer who forgets, but a doer who acts, he will be
blessed in his doing" (James 1:25).

9

LOVE AND SUFFERING

Suffering

Rain poured in spurts as the sun shone through the clouds making several rainbows appear in the sky. The drive from Dallas to Galveston is about five hours when traffic was clear, and this Friday in the middle of October proved to be a smooth drive down to the coast.

Originally, I had turned down the offer to go to the coast with my sister and her two eldest sons, but after I had to leave work early because of another anxiety attack, I decided that I needed to get away. These anxiety attacks had to stop, but I wasn't even certain what was causing them. However, a weekend away sounded like a great idea.

A few hours later found me on the beach across from the hotel on Galveston island. My sister was sitting in the shade under one of the docks as her two sons played in the sand and took turns walking out into the waves.

As evening began to approach, I excused myself from them and walked down the sandy beach. The beach, mostly clear of pedestrians, was instead, filled with other types of life.

A flock of small birds chased the waves looking for food. Some of the larger birds circled overhead watching for bigger prey. A small sand crab waddled across the path as it headed for home for the evening. But even more beautiful to see was the sand littered with small sea shells that reflected the sunlight on this mostly clear evening creating an illusion of gems everywhere you turned.

Beauty surrounded me everywhere, and for the first time in almost two years, I actually allowed myself to enjoy it. That evening, as I walked along the sandy bank, I took some time to actually listen. The phrase "be still, and know that I am God" was floating through my mind over and over again, and I realized that my biggest problem was that I wasn't allowing myself to be still and listen.

So, over the next two days, I took some time to actually stop and listen to God. I spent some time in the Bible and other time just watching my nephews enjoy the beach. But most importantly, it was this trip to the beach where I began to seek God again, and it was the first real steps I made toward healing.

As a practicing Christian, one of the hardest internal battles I faced had to do with the merging of God's character (that He is both God of love and a God of justice) with the idea that He allows us to suffer things (sometimes horrible things) that are not a direct result of our own sin. Considering my early exposure to real suffering that didn't seem to connect to any choice I personally had made, I had to work through this at a fairly early age.

Working to coalesce these two concepts in my mind took years of my life.

Suffering is such a complex issue that I couldn't tell you everything about it. I can only tell you what I have discovered both biblically and from life experience. In my mind's eye, suffering fits into one of three major categories. There is suffering which is a direct result of our sin—suffering for instruction. There is suffering that is the direct result of our righteous behavior—attacks from the enemy. And then, there is suffering that is not as easily identified or categorized because, in our limited view on Earth, we don't know the source or reasons behind it—I have grown to think of this type of suffering as "trials by fire." To fully understand suffering, we have to first address each of these topics individually, and then consider them as a whole.

Suffering as Instruction

While most of the healings in the New Testament are a testament of faith—which I discuss in the chapter on grace and the chapter on faith—a select few were specifically tied to forgiveness of sins. In Matthew chapter 9, Mark chapter 2, and Luke chapter 5, we are given a short narrative of one such healing. This particular narrative is a critical one for both us and the Jews of Christ's time because it impacts our understanding of both Christ's teachings and His power. Read for yourself the story as it's written by Matthew:

> "And getting into a boat he crossed over and came to his own city. And behold some people brought to him a paralytic, lying on a bed. And

when Jesus saw their faith, he said to the paralytic, 'Take heart, my son; your sins are forgiven.' And behold some of the scribes said to themselves, 'This man is blaspheming.' But Jesus, knowing their thoughts, said 'Why do you think evil in your hearts? For which is easier to say, "Your sins are forgiven," or to say, "Rise and walk"? But that you may know the Son of Man has authority on earth to forgive sins'—he said to the paralytic—'Rise, pick up your bed and go home.' And he rose and went home" (Mt 9:1-6).

We don't know the specific circumstances that led to this man's paralysis—whether it was the direct result of a specific sin or a general result of overall sin—and, to the case at hand, it seems irrelevant. What we can know is that the forgiveness of sins was, in fact, the key to his healing here. This suffering that he experienced was likely the result of his own sin, and therefore a consequence of his own behavior and choices.

It's easy to understand this type of suffering because it seems "fair" to us. If a man commits a murder, there should be consequences. If a person steals from a store, then there are consequences. Those consequences are often not pleasant for the person, but even the one on the receiving end of the suffering, on some level, understands that it was their own choice to cause this suffering for themselves. Being such an easy concept, you might wonder why I'm even spending time on it, so let me get to the point.

In our society today, which focuses on "being yourself" and not letting anyone tell you who you are, it's very easy for Christians to fall into the idea that we are under

God's grace, and therefore free of any punishment for sins that we commit. That's not actually true, and some of the proof of that has been quoted in various chapters of this book, so I won't go off on that rabbit trail. Punishment is used for correction, not vengeance, which is a method of instruction and if we ignore the suffering we have that is a punishment, then we cannot be instructed. The anxiety attacks I was suffering directed me to examine myself and my life, and to correct my direction before it was too late. Those attacks were a direct result of my own sin even if the anxiety itself was born out of suffering that was not my fault. Had I refocused on God earlier, I may never have suffered in such a way, but I ignored all of His earlier calls, so He sent a stronger call my way. And don't forget, "whoever ignores instruction despises himself, but he who listens to reproof gains intelligence" (Prov 15:32).

Let me give you an easy-to-understand example. When I moved out on my own for the first time, and I had my own apartment, of course, I thought it was cool that I could order pizza whenever I wanted, I could stay up late and watch TV and no one complained, and so many other things that are nice about living alone. After not too long living on my own, I noticed that some nights I was having severe stomach cramps, and I wouldn't be able to go to sleep until three or four in the morning. After a while, I started asking myself why that was happening, and I began to notice a pattern. Whenever I ate pizza, I would get sick to my stomach. Later, I made the connection with dairy, and I realized that I'm intolerant. If I had never stopped to ask myself why this was happening, I would still be dealing with this even today—as a matter of fact, one of my siblings suffered silently with the same cramps for years without considering causes, and once I pointed out the connection I made, they made the same one and have been cramp free for just as long. In the same way, I had ignored all of the attempts of God to get my attention until I started suffering anxiety attacks that were nearly debilitating. The result was, shall we say, unpleasant.

If we don't stop and ask ourselves if the suffering we are going through is connected to our own sin, then we will never grow as a Christian, and we will stagnate. It may even cause us to lose some of our faith in God because the suffering will come again and again just as those cramps did for my sibling. We don't want to be the child who burns himself by touching the hot stove and then reaches out to touch it again.

Attacks from the Enemy

Then, there is another kind of suffering. This suffering can be some of the most devastating if you're not prepared for it. It comes when we *are* doing the right thing and making choices to serve God. It comes from outside of us and is often malicious in intent. This is the suffering that is a direct attack of the enemy.

It might appear in the form of being ostracized by friends because you "believe that outdated religious stuff." Also, it could be the loss of a job because you live your faith, and your boss doesn't want that "religion" at his business. It could also come in the form of "excommunication from a church" because you pointed out the blasphemy that was seeping into their doctrine. There are many ways that the enemy chooses to attack, but you must be aware that he does attack, and he attacks when you're seeking God the most.

Peter warns us about these attacks from the enemy in his first letter when he says, "Be sober-minded; be watchful. Your adversary the devil prowls around like a roaring lion, seeking someone to devour. Resist him, firm in your faith, knowing that the same kinds of suffering are being experienced by your brotherhood throughout the world" (I Pet 5:8-9). This would be a pointless warning if the devil had lost his teeth as I have heard claimed in some circles. The devil can, and will, attack us at any given opportunity. But, we're not just told to resist, we are given tools to resist as well. Paul, in his letter to the Ephesians, provides for us some of the most complete and concise directions for resisting the devil:

> "Finally, be strong in the Lord and in the strength of his might. Put on the whole armor of God, that you may be able to stand against the schemes of the devil. For we do not wrestle against flesh and blood, but against the rulers, against the authorities, against the cosmic powers over this present darkness, against the spiritual forces of evil in the heavenly places. Therefore take up the whole armor of God, that you may be able to withstand the evil day and having done all, to stand firm" (Eph 6:10-13).

Following this introduction, Paul outlines for us what the armor of God is: belt of truth, breastplate of righteousness, shoes—the readiness given by the gospel of peace—shield of faith, helmet of salvation, sword of the Spirit which is the Word of God. This suffering is very real and can be some of the hardest we go through in life. Our best defense against it is a firm foundation in our faith. If we are truly and firmly convinced that Christ came, lived and died for our sins, and was resurrected and now sits on the throne in heaven, then we know that we cannot be defeated here on earth. Even if we lose a battle, the war is already won.

I have noticed that when I am trying to get closer to God and to seek His will over my own, that's when I begin to have problems completely outside of myself. My internal world is strongly seeking God, but my job, some of my friends, my car, my health, that's when it all seems to be under the greatest attack. This year, it seems the whole world is under attack, but I know that my redeemer lives (Job 19:25), and in Him, I can have absolute faith and trust.

Trials by Fire

The final kind of suffering that I have experienced and witnessed is that of the suffering that doesn't appear to have any direct cause. In my head, I have always referred to this suffering as "trials by fire." This refers to all suffering that, in our heads and hearts that seek and trust the Lord, doesn't seem to make sense. The horrible tales we hear of babies being thrown in trash cans, of children innocent and naive experiencing extreme abuse, of the victims of sex slave trade, and so much more. How do we explain this? As I have struggled with it, I have found two truths about this suffering: (1) It is suffering that exists because we live in a sinful and debauched world where men have free will; and (2) this suffering is used as a direct (to those specifically involved in the suffering) and an indirect (to those who know of the suffering before, during, or after) refiner's fire.

Let's address the second truth first. Several times, God talks about refining His people, such as in Zechariah when He says, "And I will put this [final] third [of sheep] into the fire, and refine them as one refines silver, and test them as gold is tested. They will call upon my name, and I will answer them. I will say, 'They are my people'; and they will say, 'The Lord is my God'" (13:9).

In the final chapter of *Mere Christianity*, Lewis talks about "The New Men" and how we become these men. It's not an easy thing to change ourselves, for our old self to die and be reborn. Both birth and death are difficult in the physical realm, and so, it works out that they are both difficult in the spiritual realm as well. Without the refining fire, we can't burn off the remaining dross of the "old us" and then we would be but an imperfect vessel that would break under pressure. God promises us perfection, and this is one of the things we have to go through to reach that goal.

Going back to the first truth, this is the harder cause of suffering for us to address. We live in a sinful world, and sometimes, innocent people are hurt in some of the worst ways because of that reason alone. While the suffering often has the benefit of acting as a refining fire, there is nothing in us that allows us to say that a just God, a God who is loving, would cause this. How can God, who is all-powerful and all-knowing, let such things happen? How could He let a small child be hurt after declaring His love for them? Shootings, rapes, beatings, torture, war, and so much more plagues our world constantly. How do we come to terms with this? It's not an easy job, for certain.

Theologically explaining it is almost like defining gravity. While the effects of gravity are known and accepted, explaining the details of what causes those effects are unknown and, currently, unexplainable. There are theories, but no real and absolute knowledge. All I can share on this topic is my personal theory and why I hold to this theory.

As discussed earlier in this chapter, we are currently at war. The devil is prowling around looking for people to swallow up. Anyone who is not making use of their shield of faith and their sword of the Spirit may find themselves a victim to the devil's whims. But, much like in a real war, sometimes even people who are using their shields and weapons may find themselves injured by a well-performed shot of the enemy.

We are not the ones being attacked, God is. Because we have sided with God, then we become targets as well. But even God, when He went to save Lot from the destruction of Sodom, was under attack there. The men came to Lot to demand that he turn over the "strangers" to them so that they could "know" them—a euphemism for rape (Gen 19:4-5).

This suffering comes as a natural result of the spiritual warfare that we are engaging in. Currently, we are on the front lines of the war standing between the devil and God's kingdom. We know God has won the war, the decisive battle has already been won, but we are still freeing God's territory of the enemy's spies, soldiers, and general influence. When we stand between the devil and his attempts to take back what God has already won, we, much like Lot, will find ourselves being targeted right along with the victor (Gen 19:9).

Love and Suffering

Each bit of suffering that we experience in our lives is not one or the other of these three categories, but rather, it is a conglomerate of all three in different parts. God, unlike a human king, has won the war, and He is placing everything into the perfect spot so that all things will work together for the good of those who love Him (Rom 8:28)—again, not for the good of all mankind.

Job, a righteous man who sought God with his whole self and did what was right and good, that even Satan could not find fault with, experienced suffering the likes of which many of us have never even come close to. He had absolute faith beyond what most of us can brag, and yet ... even he was attacked. In the battle between Satan and God, Job became an attractive potential conquest because he had taken God's side and had done it well. If Job fell, then it was proof that man wasn't worth God's time or effort. (It is even pointed out later that there was no specific sin he needed to repent of as his friends had suggested from when God rebuked those friends.)

He lost his wealth, his children, and his own health, and none of it had to do with his own sin. Now, he, unlike many of us, did in fact examine his own heart. In Job 9, we see that he has considered his own life and sin, and while he found sin, he could not find a specific sin that could be corrected through instruction from the Lord in this fashion. Being that God is a just and wise God, bringing great calamity on Job for general sins that we all commit on a daily basis doesn't seem to be a useful tool for instruction. But, while this appears to be true at the beginning, Job is, in fact, instructed through this experience. In chapters 38-41, God addresses Job and instructs him about His character and being. After everything, we can see that Job suffers for all three reasons; he suffered attacks from the enemy, trials by fire, and as instruction from God.

And let us never forget the strongest tie between love and suffering is that the greatest act of love recorded in human history was done through suffering. For our faults, our sins, our rebellion and pride, God came down and took on flesh and suffered injustice, ridicule, rejection, physical pain, torture, and even death. Nothing required Him to do such a thing, and yet, because He is love, He did. So, if God is love, and God works all things together for the good of those who love Him, and God is all-powerful and all-knowing, then it must be true that suffering, regardless of the reason for it, is done for our benefit and our good.

I think that the best way to end this is with Peter's words about suffering in the Christian life:

> "Beloved, do not be surprised at the fiery trial when it comes upon you to test you, as though something strange were happening to you. But rejoice insofar as you share Christ's sufferings, that you may also rejoice and be glad when his glory is revealed. If you are insulted for the name of Christ, you are blessed, because the Spirit of glory and of God rests upon you. But let none of you suffer as a murderer or a thief or an evildoer or as a meddler. Yet if anyone suffers as a Christian, let him not be ashamed, but let him glorify God in that name. For it is time for judgment to begin at the household of God; and if it begins with us, what will be the outcome for those

who do not obey the gospel of God? And 'if the righteous is scarcely saved, what will become of the ungodly and the sinner?' Therefore let those who suffer according to God's will entrust their souls to a faithful Creator while doing good" (I Pet 4:12-19).

10

LOVE AND FAITH

Faith

We discussed faith already once in this book when we talked about grace, the free gift of God, but I want to talk about faith in larger terms. More precisely, I want to address what faith is, what it looks like, and how we can use it as a shield as Paul tells us in his letter to the Ephesians. I also want to address faith as it pertains to love both from us to God and from God to us.

Before we go too much further, let's look at faith as it's defined in the Bible. The author of the epistle to the Hebrews tells us that "faith is the assurance of things hoped for, the conviction of things not seen" (Heb 11:1). As the infallible Word of God, we can trust that is the whole truth of the matter, and that itself is a demonstration of faith. I would argue that faith and trust are synonymous with each other. Considering what we talked about with suffering, the conclusion there was that God works "all things together for the good of those who love

Him" (Rom 8:28). If we have faith that this is true, then no matter what we are suffering in the present moment, we trust that's true and therefore, we trust God above all else. That trust is faith.

As a child, I was taught that faith was the belief in things not seen, but it's more than just that. Remember, "even the demons believe—and shudder!" (James 2:19). Belief on its own is not enough. We must have absolute assurance and conviction that these things are true and absolute *and* we must trust that God is love and He loves us. Trust is the difference between *belief* and *faith*.

It is absolutely true that Jesus Christ is God (Jn 8:58). It is absolutely true that He died and was resurrected (see all four gospels). It is absolutely true that we are sinners (Rom 3:23). It is absolutely true that we need a redeemer (Col 1:14). We accept these truths as absolutes, and we are thoroughly convinced that they're true, and we put our trust and hope in these truths. That is much more than just a surface level "belief" that Christ existed and was a "great man" as I've heard Him described by some.

When we, as people, accept these things as true at the deepest level of our being, they change us. We begin to see our sin for what it is: dirty, disgusting, and devastating to ourselves and to God. We begin to start stepping toward God and with His help, moving in a direction that takes us out of the shadows and into the light. "God is light" (I Jn 1:5), and our faith allows us to see, enjoy, and be in that light.

Faith's Appearances

But, faith is not a new thing reserved only for those born after Christ's death and resurrection. Faith dates back to the beginning of time with Cain and Abel, and we have a good recorded summary of what I mean in Hebrews 11, the "faith" chapter of the New Testament. This chapter addresses Abel's faith in his offering to God which bestowed favor on him. Abel suffered because he was in the light, and the darkness hates the light, so he was slain by his brother's envy, but his faith is still commended thousands of years later.

The author also talks about Abraham's faith, Sarah's faith, Isaac's faith, Jacob's faith, and the faith of Moses and the people as they crossed the Red Sea. None of these people witnessed the fulfillments of God's promise to them, but they did however have absolute conviction that the promises were going to be fulfilled: "And all these, though commended through their faith, did not receive what was promised since God had provided something better for us, that apart from us they should not be made perfect" (Heb 11:39-40). What does faith look like? It looks like absolute assurance that the promises we have will be kept. It looks like absolute trust in the goodness of God.

We are incapable of maintaining faith without some aid, though. Jesus is described shortly after these verses (which proclaim the faith of the forefathers) as being the "founder and perfecter of our faith" (Heb 12:2). Faith in these promises is not an easy assurance, but one that we have to fight to maintain and keep. It is the continuous trust in the things that we ourselves didn't have the privilege to witness, and therefore, it is a trust that has to be fed and preserved over time.

We, as people, are forgetful. Think about your own day-to-day life. How often are you in the middle of a thought, and you completely forget what you're saying?

Or, how many times do you walk into a room and have no memory of why you went in there? Or, better yet, how well do you remember that nice stranger from twelve years ago who made you smile in line at the grocery store? I know that these are memory struggles that I have. The problem is that forgetful people do "not remember His power or the day when He redeemed them from the foe" (Ps 78:42). We're warned about this back in the writings of Moses when he says to "take care, and keep your soul diligently, lest you forget the things that your eyes have seen, and lest they depart from your heart all the days of your life. Make them known to your children and your children's children" (Deut 4:9).

As a forgetful people, there are two steps to maintaining our faith, and each is useful to help with the other.

First, our life's mantra should be "Thy Word have I hid in my heart that I might not sin against Thee" (Ps 119:11 KJV). If we immerse ourselves in God's promises all the time through the study and memorization of God's words, then it would be hard to forget His promises to us. This is not me preaching to you and telling you what you should and should not do. Rather, it's me speaking in solidarity with you about that which we both should aim to do. I, by no means, am perfect at this, and often I lose the habit, but I can say from personal experience that each time I come back to it, the richness of my life increases. As Paul said, "Faith comes from hearing, and hearing through the word of Christ" (Rom 10:17). We should always strive to seek out God's word, and some ways we can do that is through church, through relationships, *and* through our own Bible studies—note that I said *and*, not *or*, because we should do all three.

Just a bit of a side note to those who would say that they can have a good worship of God in their home without having to support the "institution." Church is important because it helps us to remember. We are told to "consider how to stir up one another to love and good works, not neglecting to meet together, as is the habit of some, but encouraging one another, and all the more as you see the Day drawing near" (Heb 10:24-25). We are not supposed to neglect meeting other Christians for several reasons (I could write a whole book on that topic alone, but that's for another time), but in this passage specifically, we are told to use it to stir each other up in love and good works. If we're not around others, who is there to love? Who is there to receive our good works? How are we able to seek out time to show God's love to others? We are supposed to be with each other to facilitate the keeping of God's commands.

And second, we can remember God's promises to us through the use of a consistent yearly calendar of Christian holidays. For many years of my life, I did not have a good grasp of what we consider the Christian calendar. Of course, I knew Christmas and Easter and what they represent, but I didn't understand Pentecost or any of the other Jewish holidays. Even now, I don't believe I have a full enough understanding of them all that I could break them down for you, but I do recommend that you pursue that knowledge because it has proven to be highly beneficial to me. I also recommend celebrating Easter and Christmas; not necessarily in the way the world does with Santa and eggs, but rather in a reverent way that truly gives these holidays the solemnity and beauty that they deserve.

Shield of Faith

Now that we've talked about faith's appearance and maintenance, let's talk about it as a shield from our enemy. While a handful of miracles performed by Christ mentioned the forgiveness of sins, most of them accredited faith as the source of healing. "Your faith has healed you" seemed to be Christ's response time after time in each of the gospels' records of His healing miracles. Each of these people were under a constant physical bombardment of attacks from the enemy, and their healing came when their absolute assurance of God's promises planted itself firmly in front of them which stopped the flaming arrows immediately. Faith is a powerful shield, and it would take an equally powerful attack from the devil to get past it.

Christ's words on faith give us a greater understanding of this when He says, "Truly, I say to you, if you have faith and do not doubt … if you say to this mountain, 'Be taken up and thrown into the sea,' it will happen. And whatever you ask in prayer, you will receive. If you have faith" (Mt 21:21-22). Faith is the backbone of our life as Christians and provides for us all of the tools necessary to stand against the enemy in front of us. (Now, don't take things out of context. The quote above was given directly to the apostles, and not to all men. Also, there is a misguided belief that "if you have enough faith" you will win the lottery because you prayed for it. That's not true. The truth is, something like that could actually be very detrimental to your spiritual walk, and so often, it doesn't happen. We know that God works all together for our good, that is, our spiritual good.)

As a shield against the enemy and all of his agents, faith finds its greatest power. Let's consider some *modern* situations where faith can protect us from the enemy. One of the greatest modern tools of the enemy to attack us is social media. Both believers and unbelievers find it easy to fully expose their dark side on social media and to attack others behind the safety of their computer screen. As a high school teacher, I see some of the worst examples of this that you can imagine. We so often think that since we're not right in front of someone, then we are safe from them, but I have found that social media is the root of a lot of my anxiety and fear for many people. But, when confronted with these attacks, we have a few options. First, we can give into the fear and anxiety and mouse up—this is my first inclination. Or, we can put our faith in God who is in control and turn it all over to Him. While the second option doesn't come as naturally as the first, it has proven to be the most effective tool for me personally.

Another place we can use faith as our shield is in politics. We live in a country where each person holds a certain amount of accountability for the way the government is run. It's very easy for us to sit back and "armchair quarterback" those in the government, but we are, to an extent, responsible for the actions of our government. Faith allows us to pray and ask for guidance, and to find assurance in that guidance that, no matter the outcome, God is in control and all will be well for His people. Faith allows us to talk to those who don't agree with us with respect for their opinions, and to stand firm because we have an external standard for moral truth. We don't have to worry or be anxious, we are guarded from those flaming darts, because we have faith, or absolute assurance and conviction, that God is in control.

Now, does this mean that we should see bad ideas and policies, and think "*I have faith that those are wrong, so there's no reason to engage!*" Of course not. We do have a responsibility because we live in a situation where responsibility does lie with us. We have a voice, and if we are silent, then we are as guilty of the evil that comes from our silence as the offenders themselves. If we lived in a different country under a different government with different requirements and amount of power given to us, such as God's people in China or Qatar or any other country that runs differently, that would be a wholly, distinctly separate situation and would be handled according to the situation that exists there. But in our current America, we do have to fulfill our responsibilities or answer to God for the sins we don't try to stop in the government.

Faith and Love

Connecting faith and love seems to be a bit of an obvious connection considering what we've been discussing already. Faith is the absolute conviction deep in our soul that Christ loves us and gave Himself for us. Faith allows us to take each step in the race of life with confidence knowing that "Jesus ... who for the joy that was set before him endured the cross, despising the shame, and is seated at the right hand of the throne of God" (Heb 12:2). Faith gives us the strength, endurance, and perseverance to seek God and to love Him with all our heart, mind, soul, body, and strength as we have been commanded. But, more importantly, our faith is how we are justified. It is our faith which allows God to love us.

I have a brother who is only a few months younger than I am. He struggles in life and has become dangerous to have around. He has, more than once, stolen from various family members to the point where we can't let him know where any of us live. But the larger problem is the severity and unpredictability of his temper. This is a sad state of affairs, but it's even more sad because, over the years, we have tried to reach out to him on a regular basis, but he has made himself unreachable. He won't let us love him, and it hurts us all, but it hurts my mother the most. We continue to hope and pray that God will work within his heart to change him, but only time will tell.

Right now, the earth is filled with people who are in that situation with God. They are the prodigal son; they have gone off and squandered their inheritance, and they don't seem to see that they're eating the food meant for the pigs. It is heartbreaking, and some will come home to God, but others won't. Faith is us walking down that road to home and returning to our Father. Faith is what let's our father show us His love. While I am absolutely convinced that it is God's grace that allows us to come home, I also believe that a person who doesn't believe they're loved is incapable of seeing how much they are actually loved. That seems to be a major factor in the state of our world right now. But faith allows us to see with clear eyes and hear with open ears and know that we are loved by God and we are precious to Him.

11

LOVE AND THE FAMILY

The Family

It would be wrong to write a book about love and not address the family. I'm not just speaking about romantic partners married by choice; I'm also talking about those members of your family that are there whether you want to be connected with them or not. I'm also talking about it from a biblical perspective.

Now, I must give a small disclaimer here at the beginning and explain my perspective. First, I am not now, nor have I ever been married, so this chapter is *not* an advice chapter for those who want to fix or change their marriage status. I can't tell you how to find a spouse or how to treat a spouse (except through the lens of the Bible). However, I am closely involved with my family, and I have seen several marriages that have failed, and some that have succeeded against all odds. I have been involved in the raising of children since I was a child—there was about four years of time in my life from the age of twenty to twenty-four where I was independent of the direct raising of a child. I can share my observations as an external observer, but the only expertise I claim is that which is given to me in the Bible.

Before I start, I want to define the terms of a family unit. Husband is a word I use to refer to the biological male in the marriage contract, and wife is the term referring to the biological female. I will speak of marriage as it is defined in the Scriptures as being between one man and one woman. Children refer to any child raised in the home, whether biological or adopted.

> "Then the man said, 'This at last is bone of my bones and flesh of my flesh; she shall be called Woman, because she was taken out of Man.' Therefore a man shall leave his father and his mother and hold fast to his wife, and they shall become one flesh" (Gen 2:23-4).

> "And Jesus said to them... 'But from the beginning of creation, God made them male and female. Therefore a man shall leave his father and mother and hold fast to his wife, and the two shall become one flesh. So they are no longer two but one flesh. What therefore God has joined together, let not man separate'" (Mark 10:5, 6-9). (Also see Mt 19:4-6)

> " 'Therefore a man shall leave his father and mother and hold fast to his wife, and the two shall become one flesh.' This mystery is profound,

and I am saying that it refers to Christ and the church" (Eph 5:31-2).

But, the family unit is bigger than just the physical core unit of two parents and children. It expands to include grandparents, aunts, uncles, cousins, adult siblings, and so much more. If there was time, we could discuss the family unit in several books, but I want to focus mostly on the nuclear family unit of husband/wife, parent/children, and sibling relationships and what the Bible says love looks like in those relationships.

Husbands and Wives

This is the trickiest relationship to address, one filled with conflict and dreams of everlasting love and romance, and the one I have the least direct experience with. It is also the one most people have very strong feelings about, so I will limit my comments to direct examples and biblical instructions on this relationship.

As I addressed earlier, we are working on the assumption that marriage is a relationship that is only to be entered into by one man and one woman (see above Scriptures as well as Lev 18:22). Because we claim all Scripture as the "God-breathed" (II Tim 3:16) infallible Word, then we must also accept this as the infallible righteous "way" that we are instructed to follow.

So, let's address first the duties of the husband to the wife. Because it's said in fewer words, it is often treated almost as an after-thought in the marital relationship, but there are two main duties of the husband outlined in Ephesians chapter five. First, husbands are to be the head of the household, and second, they are to love their wives as Christ loved the church. But what does that mean?

Let's consider what Paul said in context: "For the husband is the head of the wife even as Christ is the head of the church" (Eph 5:23). I would argue that this is a huge duty and has huge implications for the husband. It would make the husband responsible for the physical, emotional, and spiritual well-being of his wife. To be the head of an organization or business makes us accountable for all actions taken by the business—both honest and dishonest to the point where we could face criminal charges for any illegal business conducted by our organization. That would be true for the head of household as well. He would have to be answerable for all of the sins and misdeeds of his family unit that are conducted under his knowledge and not corrected by him. Much as a teacher is answerable to a higher level than the student, so is the head of a unit answerable to a higher level than the unit.

And Paul further clarifies this when he says, "Husbands, love your wives as Christ loved the church and gave himself up for her that he might sanctify her" (Eph 5:25). Now, man is fallible, and God gives us grace for that, but the duty of the husband would be to, like Christ, put the well-being of his wife above his own needs even to the point of sacrificing his life for her. The magnitude of such a devotion is far greater than I can imagine, but I have seen it achieved. This is a calling, not a feeling. It's the reason that Paul says it might be better to remain single, because to marry means to devote yourself wholly to your partner—especially for men.

For women, as onerous as it may seem to fulfill your calling, the responsibility is actually so much less than it is for men. Women are called to "submit to your own husbands as to the Lord" (Eph 5:22). Women are not accountable for the whole spiritual, emotional, and physical well-being of their families in the same way that the husband is. Instead, women are told to submit, I believe, for two reasons. First, as C. S. Lewis points out in the chapter on Christian Marriage in *Mere Christianity*, they are told to submit because there has to be a "final say" on the matter. Someone has to make the decision and voting isn't an option when there are only two voting members. And second, because we are called to be a living picture of the Church's relationship with Christ, and that is a privilege and honor given solely to us as women.

Submission to husbands is such a tricky topic because the verb "to submit" has come to be associated with the idea that we should just "lie down and take whatever is thrown at you in silence be it verbal or physical abuse or otherwise damaging. He is the head and you submit to him!" That's not true, and I will be the first to argue that there is nothing biblical in such a picture. As a matter of fact, a marriage like that is, itself, a type of heresy. Submission means, once the decision has been made, that we follow it. It means that when in an adult discussion a disagreement can't be resolved to the satisfaction of both, the final say, as well as the responsibility for the consequences of the choice, comes from the husband. Submission isn't a binding of us women, it is a freeing of us. It frees us of the responsibility and all the implications of the decision.

As far as the practicality of how it should look and the real-world applications, I think Lewis did a beautiful job describing it, and I'm not sure I could do much better, but I will give the highlights. All decisions that can be, should be discussed, and partners should try to reach a decision together. Marriage is a partnership, not a tyranny, monarchy, or democracy. And, as Lewis pointed out, most (not all) women focus on the internal relations in the family (protecting and nurturing), not the external relations with the world (maturing and learning). As a teacher, I can personally attest to this: nine times out of ten, dealing with the father concerning a behavior or work issue is both more effective on motivating the student to higher goals, and less confrontational for me.

Also, women have the honor of being the picture of the Church's relationship to Christ. For many of us, it's hard to fully grasp the concept of a relationship with someone who isn't physically present with us. As women, we can show the world what the relationship between the physical church and Christ should look like. It should be a beautiful relationship where they work together to raise up generations of those who seek Christ. I do fully believe that Christ does speak to us directly both through His Word and, on occasion, through personal revelation, but also uses the Church to speak to us as well—usually in the gentler more nurturing tone, than His own. As women, that is also the part we play in the home. We are the gentler, more nurturing hand when dealing out punishments; we are often the softer correctional and instructional voice, and we are the submissive partner once a firm decision has been made. We get to be that half of the picture, and when we mess up, we disturb this beautiful picture in the same way that Moses did when he hit the rock with his rod rather than following the directions he was given (Ex. 17). While Moses was still saved, he was prevented from entering the promised land on this

Earth, and we could face similar consequences when we ignore the directions given to us to be a representation of the church.

I want to insert a quick side-note on divorce. I have by no means done an exhaustive study of the subject, and I know that it is a complicated issue including elements such as adultery, abandonment, abuse, and other more complex issues, but I do want to point out the seriousness of a divorce. Even Christ said that divorce was only written into the law of Moses because of "your hardness of heart" (Mk 10:6). Divorce only exists because of sin, and so to obtain one must be done with good godly Christian counsel and as a last resort under the situations presented. I know people who have gotten divorced because they "fell out of love" with their partner. Considering everything we have already discussed concerning what love is, I would argue that is not even a slightly biblical reason for seeking a divorce. If you are on the receiving end of such a divorce, it may be considered abandonment, but I would caution you to reconsider before seeking such a divorce.

Parents and children

Moving on from such a debated topic, let's consider the relationship parents should have toward their children. Children are a blessing from God, but such a great blessing comes with great responsibilities. Parents are called to "train up [their] child[ren] in the way they should go" (Prov 22:6a). Such a responsibility is not easy because each and every child starts at a different place and comes in with different needs and desires.

I am the fourth child of seven and I have fifteen nieces and nephews and three great nephews at this point that I am an active part of their lives when I can be. My mother's two youngest are right at a decade younger than I am, and as such, I was a regular part of their caregiving routine. I have observed children who have grown up well and ones that have struggled, and the only conclusion I can come up with is that there is no clear direction on how to do this successfully. Each child, and each group of children, are different and unique. So, the best advice is the same advice that Paul gave fathers when he said, "Fathers do not provoke your children to anger, but bring them up in the discipline and instruction of the Lord" (Eph 6:4). Parents are the picture of God to their children, and as such, they should take this seriously.

No parent does this perfectly. As a child of parents, there is some advice I can give here on how to handle the "mess ups" you will experience. First, be honest with your children. When you mess up, go to them and explain that your behavior was out of line. Some are under the mistaken idea that such an action might "undermine" parental authority. I can tell you, as a child of a person who did take such actions, that it actually strengthens your authority. When you have to do that stricter punishment that sometimes comes out as an overreaction and is—on other occasions—followed by an apology, and this time it isn't followed by an apology or reverse of punishment, it is highly impactful. As the child, I can say that it causes a deeper reflection of what I did and why it was "so bad." We will all overreact because we are human, don't be afraid to apologize for it.

I do want to put another note here. Being self-aware is important, and I can say that when I have had to apologize to students because I overreacted, it's not fun. It's humbling and I often feel a great amount of shame. But we should feel shame for our sin, and it's okay to feel that shame. Know that when you apologize to your child, you will feel shame, and it's okay. That shame will help prevent you from overreacting again later.

Remember, as parents, you are the picture of God to your children. I can tell you that my understanding of God as a father is limited because I didn't have my father for most of my life. My mother, who grew up in a hard situation, struggles to see God as a loving father because her father wasn't who he should have been when she was a child. My sister, whose father abandoned her when she was a baby, struggles connecting to God and forming a relationship because of that. Fathers are an important part of the home, and women must choose wisely when they're choosing the father of their children.

Children to the Family

Children have two sets of relationships: between them and their parents, and between each other.

The directions to children concerning their relationship with their parents are clearly outlined as far back as the ten commandments and are, in fact, carved into stone: "Honor your father and your mother, that your days may be long in the land that the Lord your God is giving you" (Ex 20:12). This is the first commandment given with a promise attached to it. Does that mean that everyone who dies young has dishonored their parents? No. We live in a world of sin where bad things do happen to good people. However, there is wisdom in this promise. Parents have knowledge and experience that they can share, and people who honor their parents often learn more than anyone can learn in a single lifetime on the basis of only their own experience.

But, what does it mean to honor your parents? As a child, it means to obey your parents. Obviously, young children don't know what will hurt them or what will help them, so this obedience is a protection put in place for the care and well-being of the children. However, as an adult, it looks different. It could mean helping to physically care for their needs, to financially provide for them, or something as simple as just regularly taking time out to talk to them and visit. Parents are worth the time, and honoring a parent means to give them time.

The relationship I have with my mother has, at times, been strained. Especially during my twenties, I let a lot of bitterness sit between us. But, since the release of that bitterness towards her and others, the resulting relationship has been my saving grace during some of my darkest times in life.

As adults, it is often easy for us to disregard this commandment because we stop thinking of ourselves as children. However, I love C. S. Lewis's very poignant point about this in his work *The Screwtape Letters*. The book is a collection of "letters" between two devils, Wormwood (the lesser devil in the field) and his commander Screwtape. The letters are addressed to Wormwood giving various directions on how to keep the newly saved "patient" from truly serving God to his full potential. The third letter is the most telling to me. It focuses on how to keep the "patient" and his mother nitpicking at each other, arguing over small things. Such a technique focuses on weakening both mother and son and prevents either from truly standing for Christ.

While it's much more devastating when things happen between children and parents because both miss out on so much information—children miss the wisdom of their parents, and parents miss the insights of their children—this kind of subterfuge (insidious bitterness and hurt feelings) is also a useful technique to use to separate siblings. Sibling relationships are interesting, and perhaps among some of the most useful "practice" relationships we ever have as people. We don't get to choose our siblings. Whether they are male or female, older or younger, quiet or loud, driven or complacent, it's all purely chance as far as how it relates to us. However, we are expected to work within that realm.

My sibling relationships are a funny thing because they range so largely in different directions. I have, as I mentioned before, a brother who has, for the moment, gone a bit off the deep end. The other five are a bit of a hodge-podge mix: one sister, who is a bit older than me, owns and operates her own business, a brother who is a gamer and works in logistics, a sister who has a Ph.D. in geology and is a stay-at-home mother with six children, and of course, my baby brother and sister who are still finding their ways in life. My relationship with each is unique in its own way, but I know, no matter what, if I'm in trouble, I can call any of them—and that has happened more than once.

However, such a set of relationships doesn't come naturally. As an adult, I spent some time examining why it is we can depend on each other like that, and I came to a realization. Growing up, my mother *explicitly* took time to teach us that it's important to be dependable and to be there for family. Short of Christ, family is the closest relationship we have on earth, and she put effort and time into teaching us that. I have also seen large sibling groups torn apart by discord and fighting that wasn't addressed, but was instead, left to fester.

My last note on this is this: parents, if you want your children to honor you, you must teach them to honor you; if you want them to love each other, you must teach them to love each other. Nothing good comes "naturally." It has to be taught. Does that mean that if you teach them, then all will turn out right? Sadly, no that's not always going to be true. Sometimes, there are other factors interfering with your child that you cannot predict or prevent, but it will lead to an overall better outcome. And, should everything go horribly wrong for a time, if you teach them right, it will make it easier for your child to come back. While this is not a promise, it is a piece of wisdom written down for our benefit: "Train up a child in the way he should go; even when he is old he will not depart from it" (Prov 22:6).

Family and Love

Just as a bit of a conclusion to all of this, I would say something about the family and love. Our family units are, in many ways, meant to mirror God's relationship with us as a race. Husbands and wives mirror the self-sacrificing relationship of Christ to the church and the submission of the church to Christ. Fathers and mothers mirror God's direct relationship with us teaching and training us in the ways we should go. Our relationship to our parents should mirror our relationship with God which should be filled with honor, respect, but also love and trust. And our relationship to our siblings should mirror our relationships with each other in Christ—being a dependable helping hand in times of distress.

A family unit working as God has outlined for us in His Word is one filled with the love of God. Does it have problems at times, and is it often imperfect? Yes. But if we seek God first, we can slowly, over time, fix each imperfection until it gets as close as we can get it to what God wants it to be while we are here on earth.

12

LOVE AND THE
EVERYDAY CHRISTIAN

Introduction

This book has discussed love on several levels—ranging from what love is to how God can be loving and still be a just and a righteous God. We've concluded that in order for us to fully love any other being, we must have God sitting on the throne of our hearts—He must be the center of our world. We've even taken a look at the importance of family as a picture of God's love for and relationship to humanity.

But, all of these are "big" ideas. We also need to talk about how it looks to be an everyday person and show the love of God.

When I read through the three Rabbi Jesus books—*Sitting at the Feet of Rabbi Jesus, Walking in the Dust of Rabbi Jesus,* and *Reading the Bible with Rabbi Jesus*—one of the many interesting tidbits I picked up is that of *gemilut hasadim*, or better known as "acts of loving-kindness." As I referenced earlier in this book, it is a part of Jewish religious culture to watch throughout the day for any chance to perform an act of loving-kindness. The way it's described in these books leaves me with the impression that Jewish culture teaches these opportunities for *gemilut hasadim*, acts of loving-kindness, have been placed in our paths on purpose to give us a chance to show God's loving-kindness. If we open our eyes and look for those opportunities, then we will find them. This chapter is a bit more practical in design, and, because of that fact, it reads a little bit differently. In each of the following sections, you will see a few stories depicting what it looks like to be an everyday Christian. The stories are true (if slightly embellished for story-telling purposes), and, in some cases, names and places have been changed.

A Friend to Friends

A Friend in Need:

Brrrrrnnnnggggg! An obnoxious sound echoed through the small store followed quickly by a crash in the back. A man could be heard swearing a bit as a man stumbled back up front to answer the phone and stop the incessant ringing.

"Yes?" A moment of silence was followed by an "I see. I'll be there soon."

Heaviness hung on Aaron's face and shoulders almost as if a pile of bricks were holding him down as he hung up the receiver. Whatever that phone call heralded, it wasn't good. He turned the open sign on the front door around so that it would read "out for lunch, be back at 2:00." He only hoped he would be back by then. Stepping out into the hot Texas sun, he shielded his face from the heat as he realized that his truck would be an oven. He turned the lock on the small hardware store door. Sighing again, he walked down a few parking spaces in the town square that had been his home for the last two decades. This would mark the third call this month, and the second time that he had to leave early. A trend was forming, and not one he was sure he was excited to see. Aaron wasn't certain what to do about it.

As he climbed into the red truck and the oven-like blast of heat settled into something a tad more tolerable, his engine roared to life. The radio seemed to scream with commercials, but the noise did nothing to distract his thoughts or ease his worries. His son was being suspended for three days. When he got back into school next week, it would be time for finals, and then summer break.

Jake was just barely fourteen, and his high school career was starting off on a bad path; Aaron wasn't sure how to change this. Jake had survived middle school with almost no problems, but these last three months of high school were not going well. What could be done? Aaron knew that the only option was to find the source of the issue.

Sometime later saw both father and son leaving the Principal Darrow's office together in silence. Hours of silence crawled on between Aaron and Jake as they went through the motions of the evening. While Aaron hadn't known before-hand the circumstances of the suspension, he understood and agreed it was the right call now. But how was he supposed to handle this with his son. If he went off too hard, he knew that Jake would shut down just like he had with his old man so many years ago.

He didn't want that. But if he just sat back, Jake would continue getting worse.

Dinner, which was normally loud and boisterous, was a strained and silent affair this night. But, as the night wore on Aaron knew that he had to address the issue. This couldn't be left alone even if it was nearly ten o'clock.

Walking into Jake's room, he considered his son whose back was facing the room and face was up against the wall. "I know it was wrong. I knew I shouldn't have done it." Aaron heard whispered from under the pile of blankets.

"Then why?" fell out of Aaron's mouth before he could even think.

"They're my friends!"

Shaking his head, Aaron sat down in the chair opposite of the bed. "That's not a friend. Friends don't purposely get each other in trouble. Friends help each other. Friends are dependable and consistent."

They sat in silence for a moment when an idea came to him. Aaron stood up and tossed Jake's shirt at the bed. "Get dressed and meet me outside in five minutes." Jake knew better than to ignore his father's request, and five minutes later, they were climbing in the cab of the big red truck. The same silence settled over them from earlier.

The drive was uneventful, but it wasn't long before they reached their destination. Aaron turned onto the gravel drive, and they went up the road for a short while, just until the house he was looking for was in sight. "Let me show you what a friend is!" he said as he pulled out his cell phone.

After a few short beeps from the phone, they both watched as lights in the house turned on, and the phone was answered.

"Hey Cecil, it's Aaron." A moment of silence passed before Aaron's real plan came out. "I'm stranded about a hundred miles north of town at the supplier's warehouse. I can't get in touch with anyone else, and I really need your help. Can you come get me?"

A moment later and the phone call was over. Jake and Aaron both watched as the man in the house, Cecil, appeared to be moving around the house, and five minutes later, was grabbing his hat as he walked out the door ... at nearly eleven o'clock at night ... to make a 200-mile round trip to help a friend.

As Cecil was walking to his truck, Aaron got out and met him to explain what was happening, but when Aaron got into the car again, he explained, "That's the kind of friend you want to have, and you want to be. A friend who is going to get you in trouble is not really a friend. But someone who will sacrifice for you as Christ did, that is a friend! Be that friend."

A Friend in Deed:

Leaving for college! What an exciting time. For hours, nearly two days as a matter of fact, we drove from Dallas to Colorado, me and my sister. She came with me to help with the drive, but soon, I knew I would be on my own, and boy was I looking forward to it. For twenty years, I lived with my family, and I really wanted some space to call my own. Just another hour and a half, and I would be getting to my new home. Sure it was only a rented room and bathroom in the home of an elderly lady, but it was going to be *my* space!

As these thoughts caused more excitement to race through my head and down my arms in tingles so sharp it made my hair stand on end, I almost missed the ringing phone. It was buried in my purse under Sarah's feet, but my sister was able to dig it out in time to answer the call. Because I was driving, she was in charge of any phone calls and directions. I heard her speak to the other person, and it was strange. Windy turns and a steep climb on the road took too much attention for me to be able to focus on the phone call, but it sounded important; however, Sarah's tone and words weren't toward family—they were a bit too respectful for that.

After she hung up, there was silence. I couldn't help it. "Well?"

"We might have a problem."

"What do you mean 'might have a problem'?" I asked suspiciously.

"That was Mrs. Henderson, the woman you're moving in with." A pause for a moment. "She said she decided she doesn't want a roommate anymore, so we shouldn't come to her house tonight."

All I remember about the minutes that followed was shock and fear. Didn't want a roommate? We had been talking for weeks. I had paid the deposit she asked for! My little sister was with me. What am I supposed to do? Where are we going to sleep tonight? I don't know anyone in Colorado. How can I fix this?

I remember that we took the next exit. There was a McDonalds up ahead, and I needed to get out of the car. We needed to make a plan. What was I going to do? For more than two hours, we sat there trying to find a place to stay, but the only thing I could afford was a campground, and we didn't have a tent. I remember going to the bathroom so I could hide my tears from my little sister. I had gotten her into this mess too.

At some point, I picked up the phone to call a friend. I needed someone to talk to. As I explained to her what had happened, Krysta quietly listened and waited for me to finish. When I was done talking, she said she needed to make a quick phone call, but she would call me back shortly. After I hung up, I sat on that toilet in the bathroom stall wondering what to do. As I left the stall, the main door opened and Sarah poked her head in to check on me.

"You okay?"

Before I could answer, though, the phone rang again. Krysta was calling me back. When I answered it, she said, "I've got a place for you to stay. I'm going to text you the address, and they know that I'm paying for this so you won't have the credit card with you. The reservation is under my name."

We talked for a few more minutes, but I know the relief was as strong, if not stronger than the shock from earlier. Sarah and I went to the hotel my friend paid for, and tomorrow didn't seem so hopeless as it had a few hours before.

A Friend to Strangers

Spencer danced with anticipation. He was headed to find his shoes because he was going to spend the whole weekend with his aunt—a whole weekend of one-on-one time where someone will let him talk about whatever he wanted. Being the oldest of half a dozen makes attention a commodity worth appreciating. As he hopped down the stairs, he saw his aunt saying goodbye to his mom, and he knew it was going to be a great weekend.

The weekend was everything he was hoping for and more. It was sunny and breezy and free of all sibling rivalry. They had watched cartoons and eaten strange foods and talked about politics—Spencer's topic of choice.

But on the last day, before going back home, his aunt let him ride along for some errands before he had to go home. Spencer didn't mind the errands because it was so easy for him to talk straight through them, but at one point, something different happened.

They were sitting at a red light, and his aunt turned to him and asked for a brown paper bag that was sitting on the floor board in front of him. Reaching down, he picked it up, and noticed that it was stapled shut with a note attached to the front of it. He didn't have a chance to read the note as his aunt took the bag and handed it out the window to a man who was holding a sign asking for food.

The light turned green, and they drove off, but Spencer's curiosity was gnawing at him. "What was that?"

"It was food."

"Food? What kind? Why did you give it to that man?"

"He needed help."

"If he needs help, why don't you give him money or a job?"

His aunt laughed as the questions seemed to pour out of his mouth while she explained, "Well, I can't give him a job because I don't have a job to give him. And I don't want to give him money because so often people in that position lose the money to bad things or bad people. Some years ago, I had a chance to have a long conversation with a homeless man. He pointed out that we should carry around food for people who live on the streets because they need it. He had lived on the streets for a few years, and he suggested that we carry these little bags with a ramen cup, a fork, and a bottle of water to give to people who need them. So, I carry them around."

After a few moments of silence, the only response Spencer could think of was "that seems like a good idea. That way we can help people who really need it."

A Friend to Enemies

A low whistle echoed around the cavern, and just like that, the moments of camaraderie were over and silent chaos ensued. Every clash of metal, every bang of wood put the whole party on edge. Fear and the need for speed traveled through the cave the same as the crashing waves on the sand.

To David, it seemed that this was taking forever, but quicker than anyone could imagine, the open area that moments earlier had been inhabited by several bodies looked as if not a single soul had entered the cavern for years. They had all managed to empty to the back parts of the cave and snuff out any hint of their presence before those coming were even close enough to see the smoke from their fires.

David would have to remember to praise his watchmen later.

Hiding in the shadows, they watched as a single man walked through the entrance of their lair. He was the worst person to have stumbled upon this spot as he was the one they were hiding from. For years he had tried to kill David and anyone who supported David's claim to the throne—a claim that was made by God, and not by David. Even now, this man, Saul, was on a campaign to find and kill him.

A few quick taps on David's shoulder and a motion or two of the hand, and David understood the message. Years together had taught them to understand even the simplest motions and communications. David quietly moved towards the man relieving himself in the front of the cave.

Here was his chance. He could end all of this chasing and insanity with a single swing of his blade. He could stop all of his suffering and go home to his wife, his friends, his family. But, as he raised the blade to end it, he found he couldn't. He couldn't take this man's life. This man was Saul, chosen by God to be the first king of Israel. What right did he have to end Saul's life?

Considering his choices, David changed direction. The king's robes were hiked up, and David was able to grab a corner of the garment and cut. He quietly moved back to the shadows.

They waited on the man to exit the cave, and after they were certain some distance separated them, David exited the cave and called to the soldiers and the king who were hunting him. Holding up the cloth, he yelled at them, "I had a chance to kill you, and I didn't. See, here's a corner of your robe, and yet, you're still alive!"

Love and the Everyday Christian

Each of these stories exemplify how we can love others—be it friend, foe, or stranger. Each story is told from a different perspective: one being helped, one helping, and one observing. We can apply each to our own lives.

This book started out as an exploration of what love is, and it ends with examples of what love can look like from life, from literature, and from the Bible. We claim Christ as our own, and as such, we should always be working to be more and more Christ-like. If we want to be as He is, then we have to sacrifice who we are. We must hand the throne in our hearts over to Him and let Him rule us.

We are everyday Christians. We live in an everyday world. We don't walk the paths of Samwise Gamgee and Frodo Baggins from *The Lord of the Rings*. We are not setting out to change the paths of history. But we do live in dark times and fight in a dark war. The fate of ourselves and those we love stand in the balance. As Tolkien pointed out several times in his epic stories, we don't get to pick the times we live in, we only get to choose how we spend that time. We can spend it bemoaning every bad thing that's happened to us and every person that's hurt us. Or, we can take up the armor God has prepared to protect us, and take up the sword that will protect those we love, and we can fight for the One who was willing to give His life for us.

How do we fight? We fight with every decision we make. Every time we pray for someone else, we strike at the enemy. Every time we act in love, we land a powerful blow against the enemy. And, every time we put others' needs in front of our own, we shine a light powerful enough to win others to Christ. So now, the battle is known, our thrones are filled, and we need to fight.

BIBLIOGRAPHY AND RECOMMENDED READINGS

1. Andrew, Sherrill, J. L., & Sherrill, E. (2017). *God's smuggler*. Minneapolis, MN: Chosen.
2. Boom, C. T. (2020). *Hiding Place, The*. S.l.: Baker Book House.
3. Eldredge, J. (2002). *Wild at heart: Field manual: A personal guide to discovering the secret of your masculine soul*. Nashville, TN: T. Nelson.
4. Eldredge, J. (2010). *Walking with God: Talk to him. hear from him. really*. Nashville: Thomas Nelson.
5. Eldredge, J. (2011). *Captivating*. Thomas Nelson.
6. Eldredge, J. (2017). *Moving mountains: Praying with passion, confidence, and authority*. Nashville: Thomas Nelson.
7. *Holy Bible: English Standard Version*. (2001). Wheaton, IL: Crossway Bibles.
8. *The Holy Bible: New international version*. (2012). Lutterworth, England: The Gideons International in the British Isles.
9. Lewis, C. S. (2012). *The great divorce*. London: Collins.

10. Lewis, C. S. (2017). *Mere Christianity*. London: William Collins.
11. Lewis, C. S. (2021). *Prince Caspian*. La Vergne: Antiquarius.
12. Lewis, C. S. (2021). *The Horse and His Boy*. La Vergne: Antiquarius.
13. Lewis, C. S. (2021). *The Last Battle*. La Vergne: Antiquarius.
14. Lewis, C. S. (2021). *The Lion, the Witch, and the Wardrobe*. La Vergne: Antiquarius.
15. Lewis, C. S. (2021). *The Magician's Nephew*. La Vergne: Antiquarius.
16. Lewis, C. S. (2021). *The Silver Chair*. La Vergne: Antiquarius.
17. Lewis, C. S. (2021). *The Voyage of the Dawn Treader*. La Vergne: Antiquarius.
18. Lewis, C. S., & Ackland, J. (2002). *The screwtape letters*. New York: HarperAudio.
19. Prager, D. (2018). *Rational Bible: Exodus*. Regnery Publishing, Incorporated, An Eagle Publishing Company.
20. Prager, D., & Telushkin, J. (2019). *The rational Bible: Genesis: God, creation, and destruction*. Washington, DC: Regnery Faith, an imprint of Regnery Publishing.
21. Spangler, A., & Tverberg, L. (2018). *Sitting at the feet of Rabbi Jesus: How the Jewishness of Jesus can transform your faith*. Grand Rapids, MI: Zondervan.
22. Tolkien J. R. R. (2007). *The Lord of the rings: Return of the king*. London: Harper Collins.
23. Tolkien J. R. R. (2012). *The lord of the rings: The two towers*. London: Harper Collins.

24. Tolkien J. R. R. (2020). *The fellowship of the Ring*. London: Harper Collins.
25. Tolkien J. R. R. (2020). *The hobbit*. London: HarperCollins.
26. Tverberg, L. (2011). *Walking in the dust of Rabbi Jesus: How the Jewish words of Jesus can change your life*. Grand Rapids, MI: Zondervan.
27. Tverberg, L. (2019). *Reading the Bible with Rabbi Jesus: How a Jewish perspective can transform your understanding*. Grand Rapids, MI: Baker Books, a division of Baker Publishing Group.